d peril. Hand hold on the wheel.

YOU ARE A TARGET MARKET

TOTAL FEMALE MALE

a **b**

RADIOHEAD
OK COMPUTER
OKNOTOK
1997 2017

New songs transcribed by Olly Weeks
Edited by David Weston & Lucy Holliday
Cover artwork and colour section by Stanley Donwood
© 2017 by Faber Music Ltd
First published by Faber Music Ltd in 2017
Bloomsbury House
74–77 Great Russell Street
London WC1B 3DA
Printed in England by Caligraving Ltd
All rights reserved

ISBN10: 0-571-54036-8
EAN13: 978-0-571-54036-5

Reproducing this music in any form is illegal
and forbidden by the Copyright, Designs and Patents Act, 1988

To buy Faber Music publications or to find out about the full range of
titles available, please contact your local music retailer or Faber Music sales enquiries:

Faber Music Limited, Burnt Mill, Elizabeth Way, Harlow CM20 2HX
Tel: +44 (0) 1279 82 89 82
fabermusic.com

RADIOHEAD
OK COMPUTER
OKNOTOK
1997 2017

4	AIRBAG
13	PARANOID ANDROID
23	SUBTERRANEAN HOMESICK ALIEN
30	EXIT MUSIC (FOR A FILM)
38	LET DOWN
43	KARMA POLICE — 48 fitter happier
50	ELECTIONEERING
58	CLIMBING UP THE WALLS
63	NO SURPRISES
69	LUCKY
74	THE TOURIST
82	I PROMISE
86	MAN OF WAR
95	LIFT
101	LULL
105	MEETING IN THE AISLE
110	MELATONIN
112	A REMINDER
119	POLYETHYLENE (PARTS 1 & 2)
124	PEARLY
128	PALO ALTO
136	HOW I MADE MY MILLIONS

AIRBAG

**Words and Music by Thomas Yorke, Jonathan Greenwood,
Colin Greenwood, Edward O'Brien and Philip Selway**

© 1997 Warner/Chappell Music Ltd
All Rights Reserved.

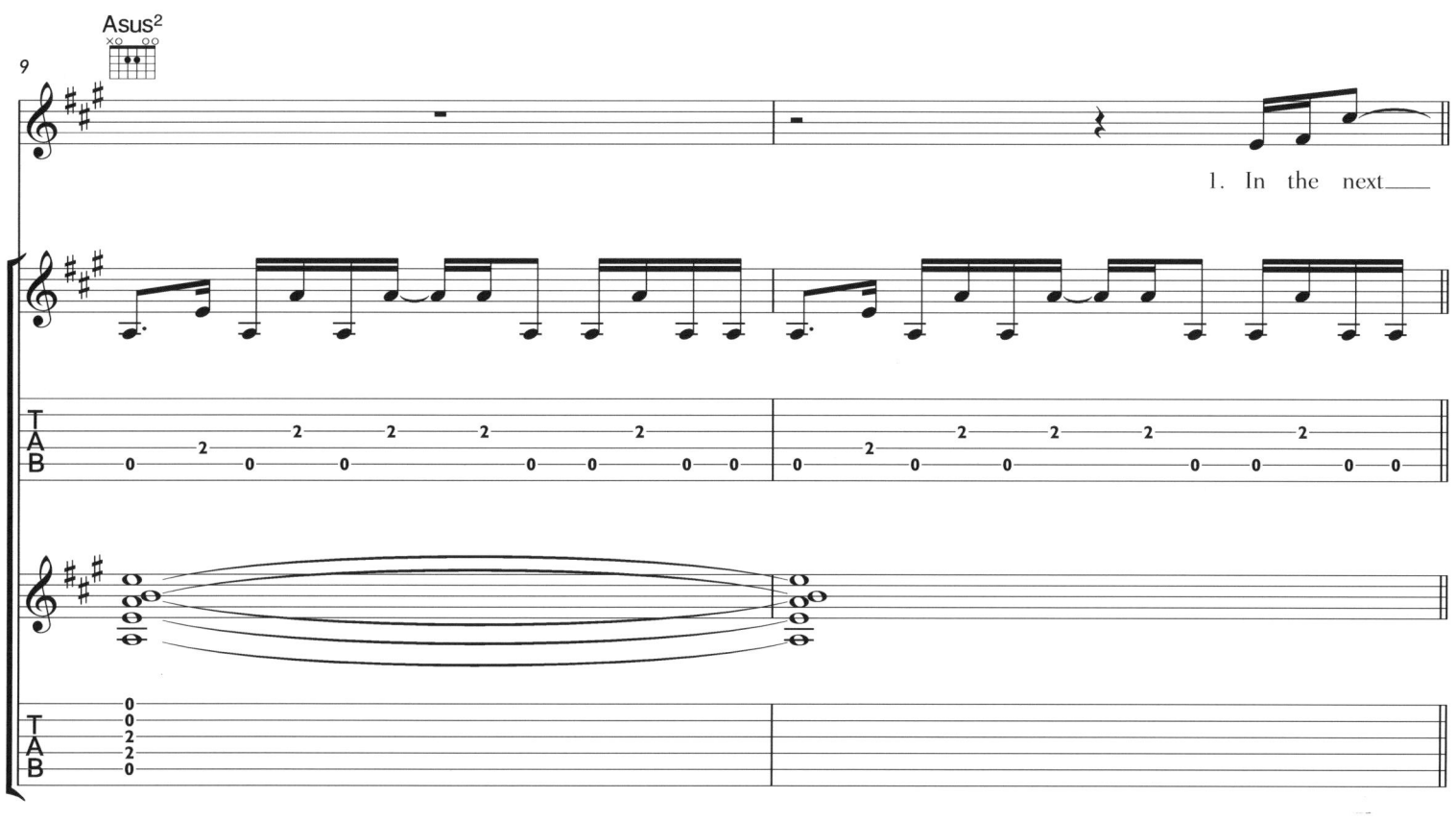
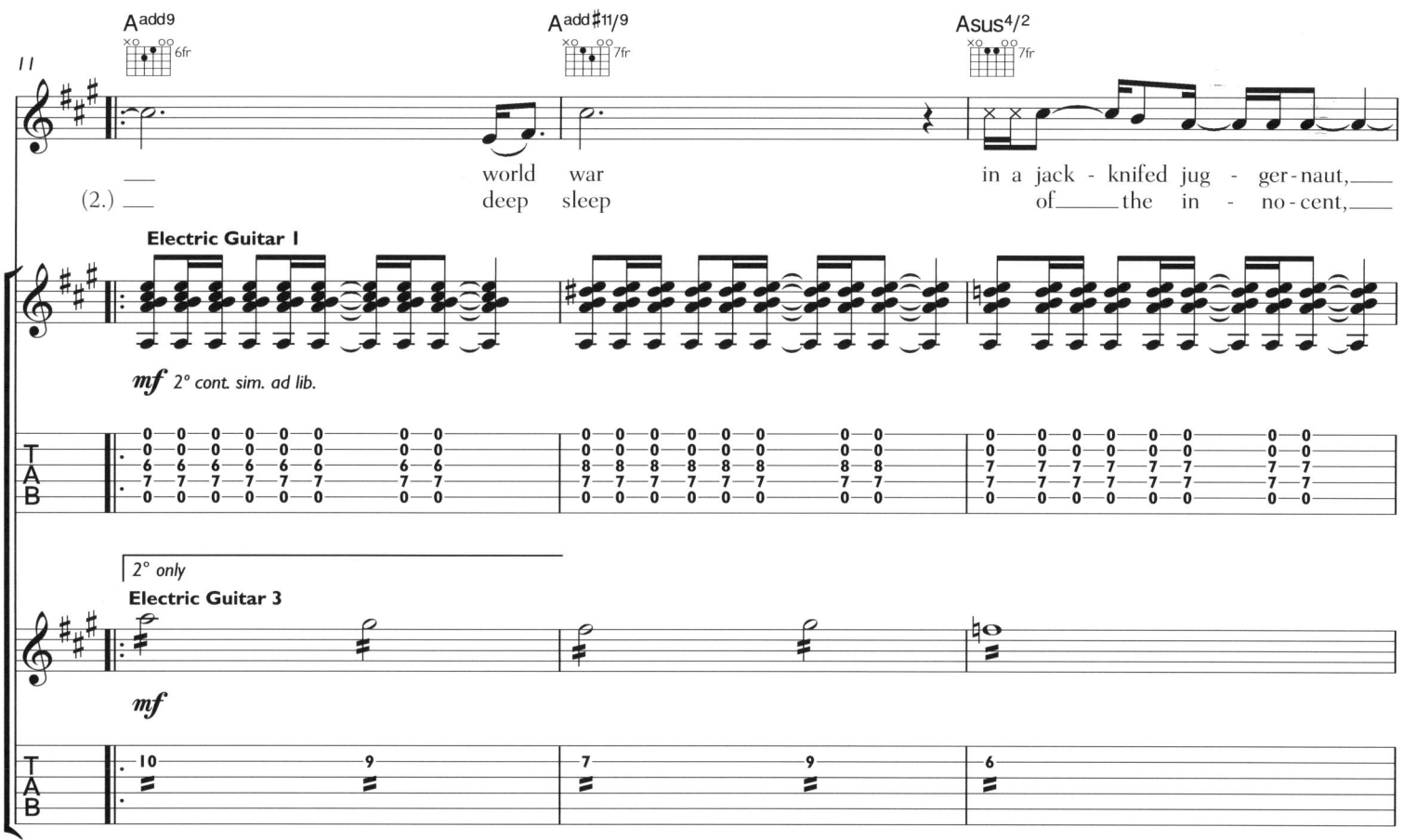

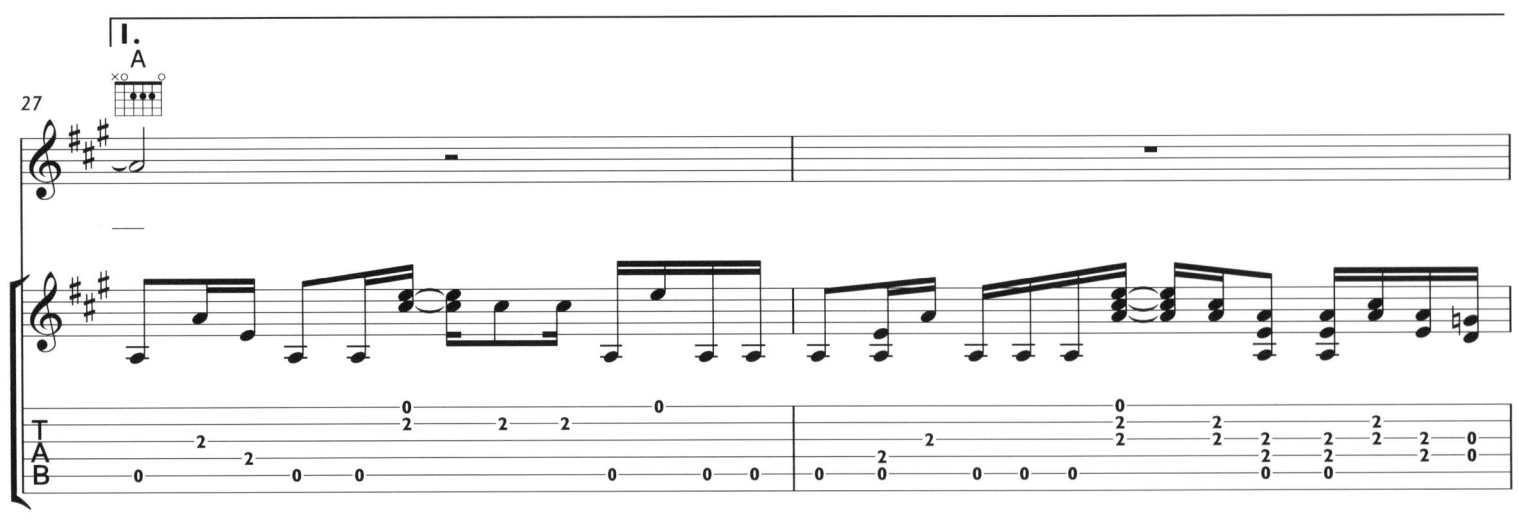
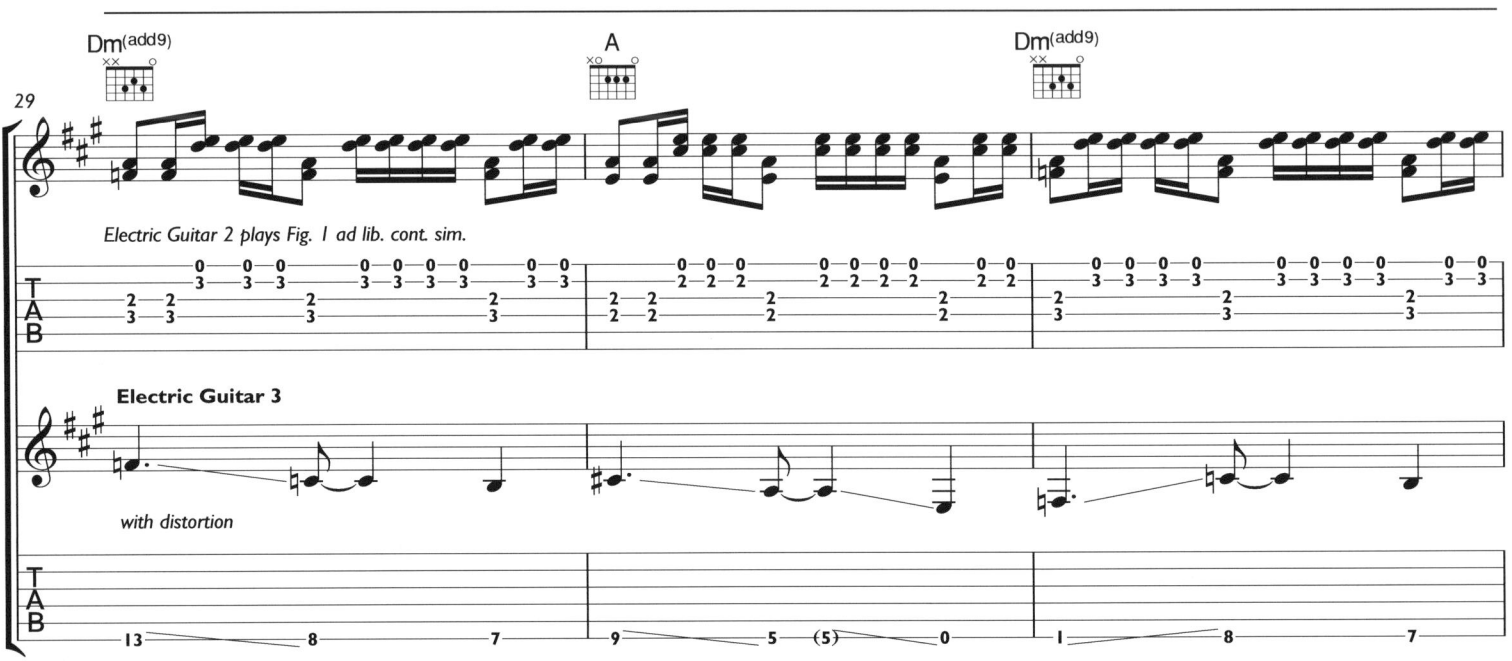
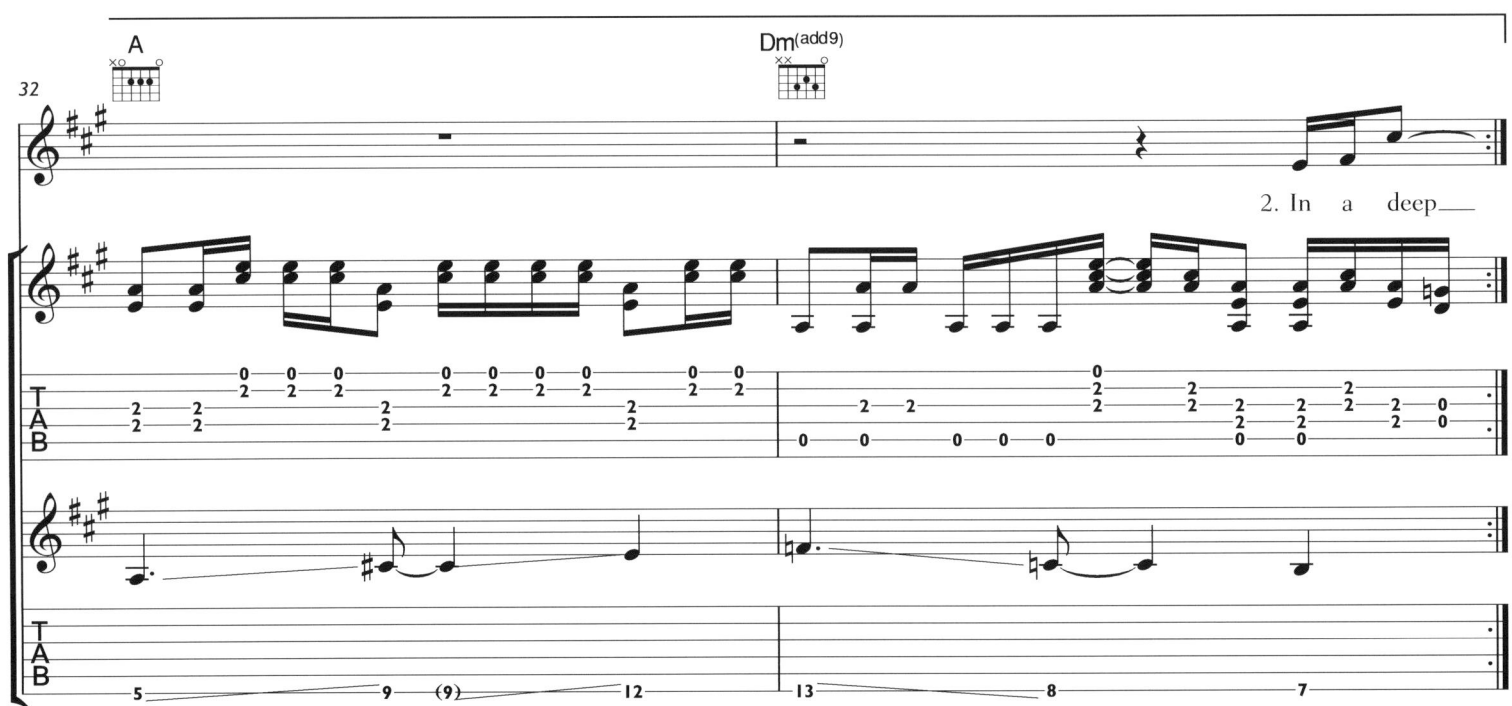

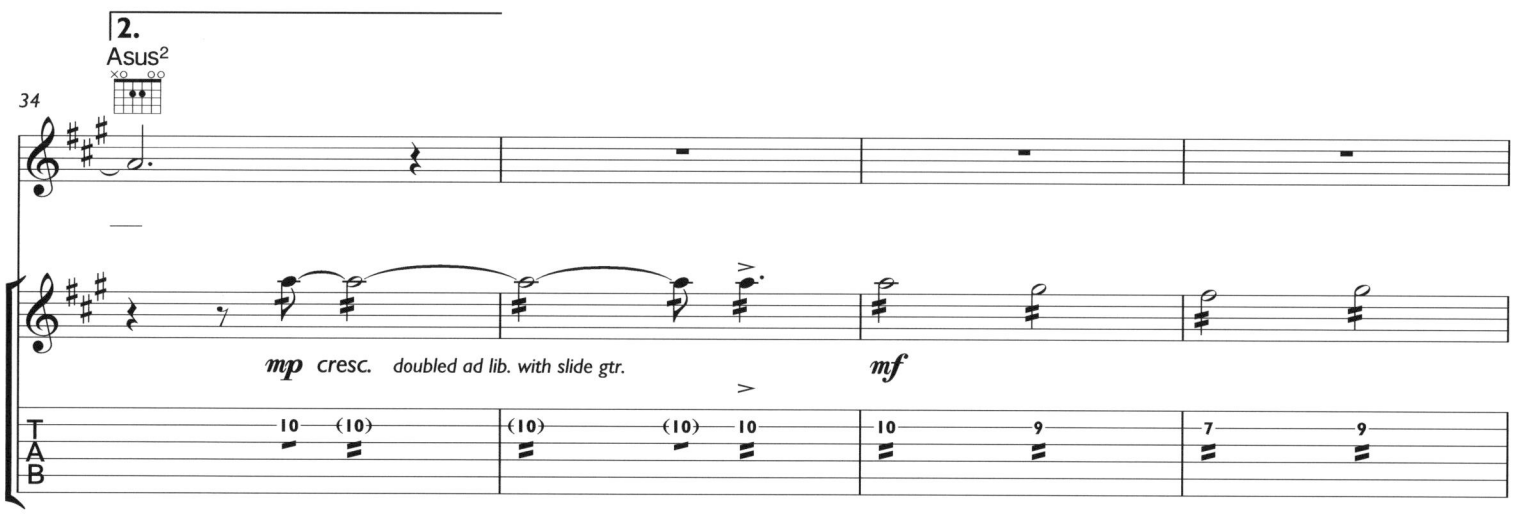
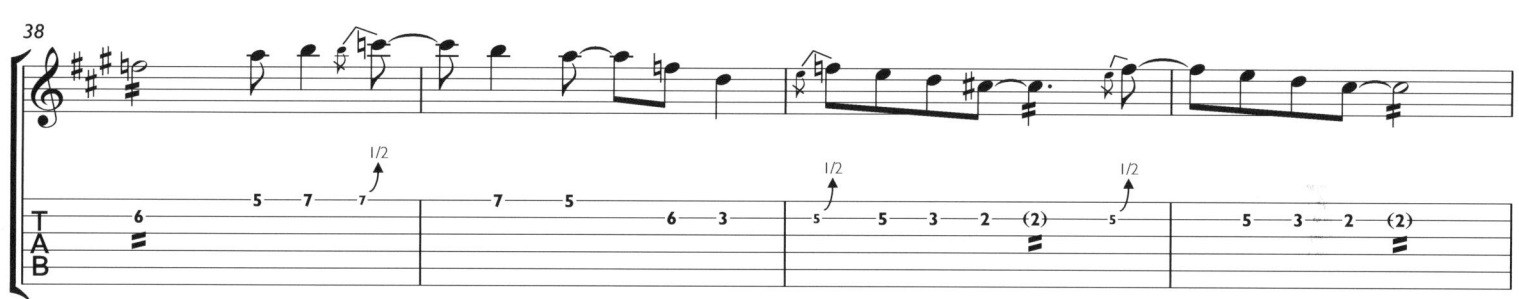

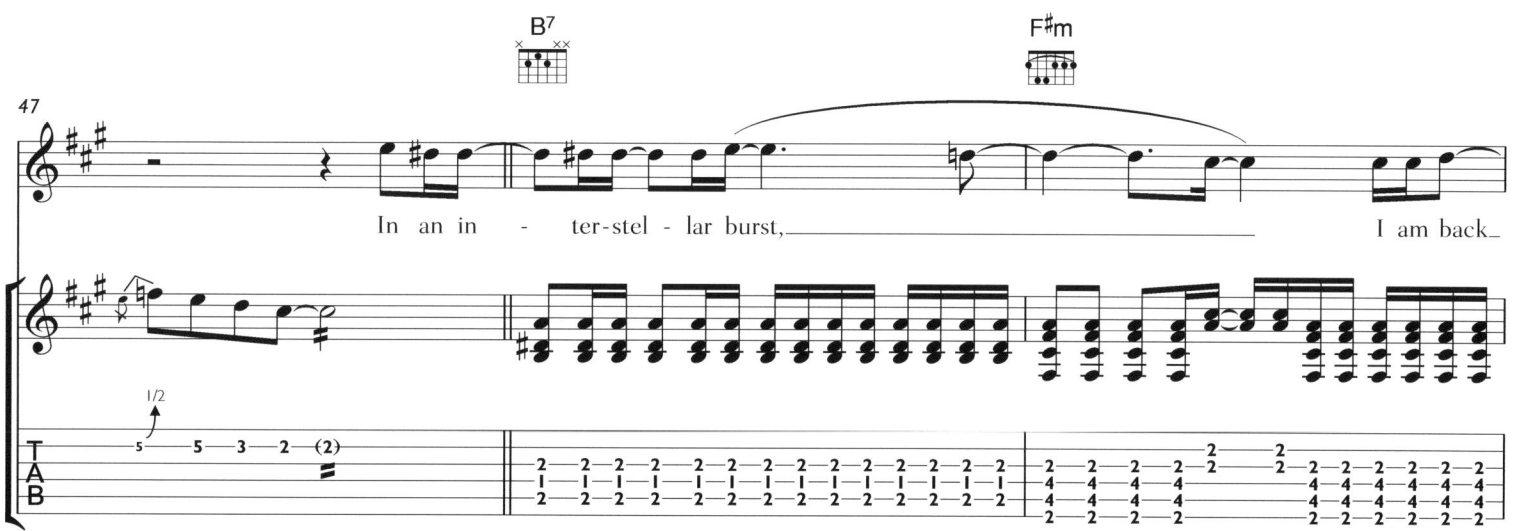

In an in - ter-stel - lar burst, I am back

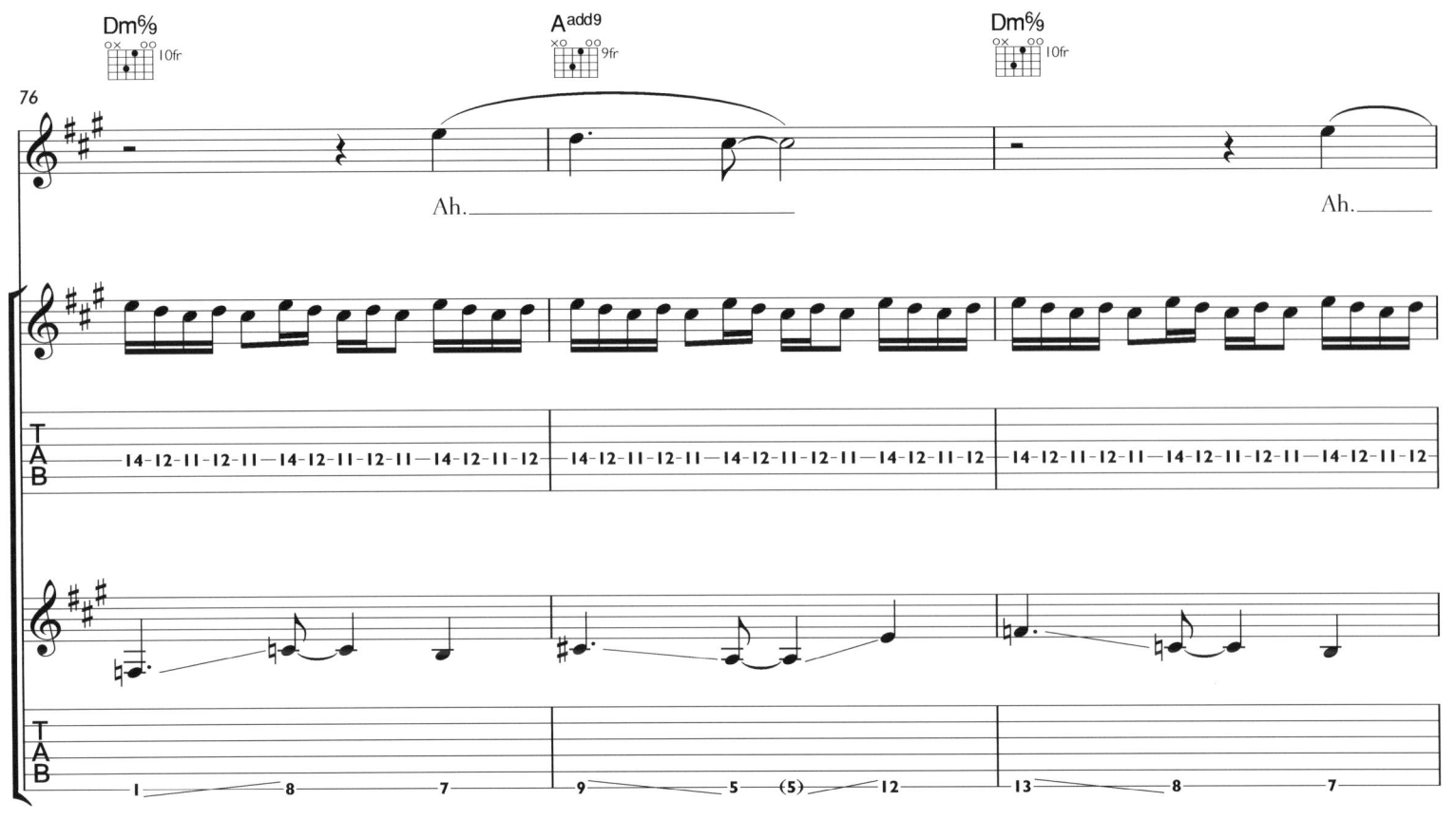
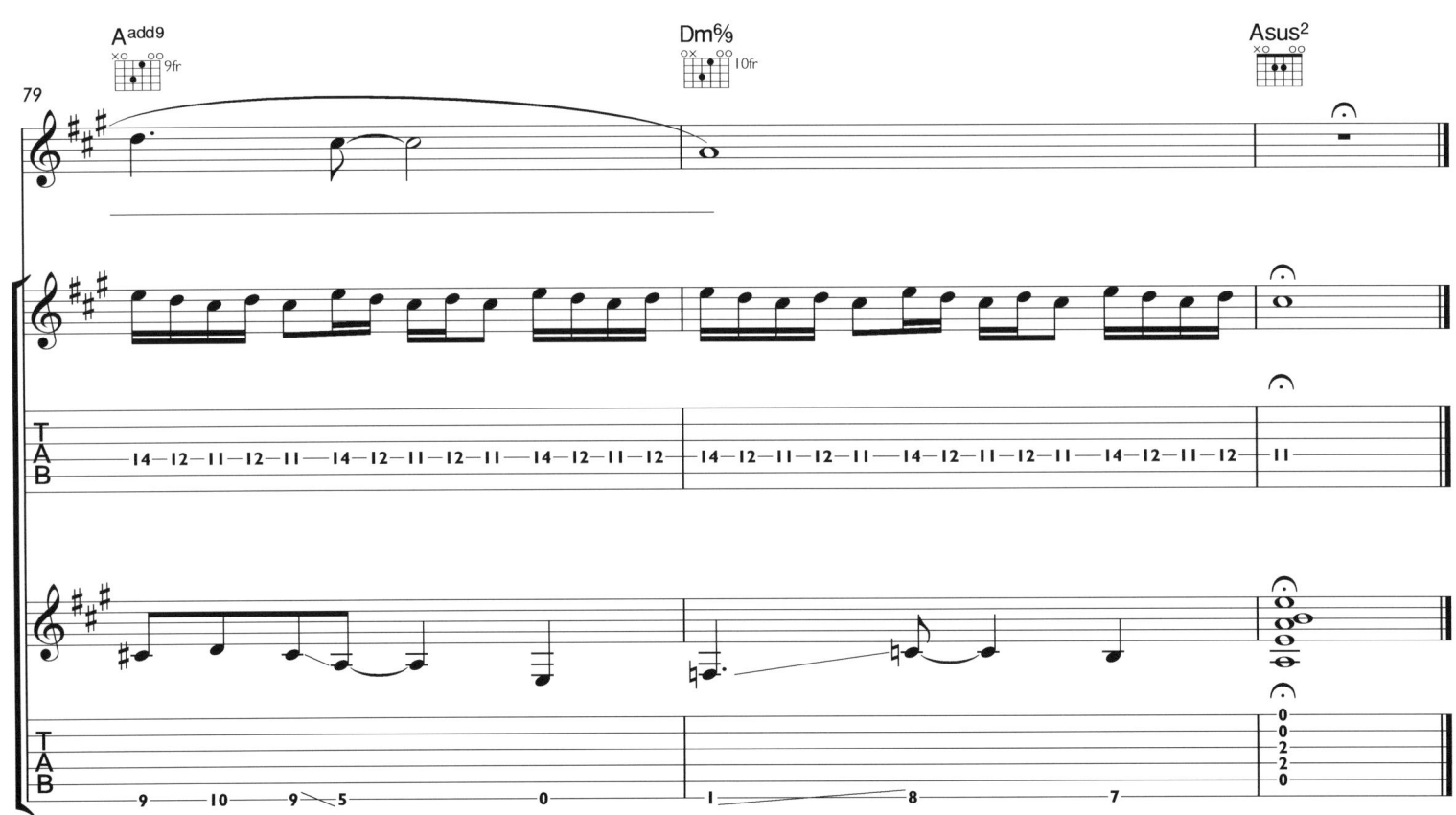

PARANOID ANDROID

Words and Music by Thomas Yorke, Jonathan Greenwood, Colin Greenwood, Edward O'Brien and Philip Selway

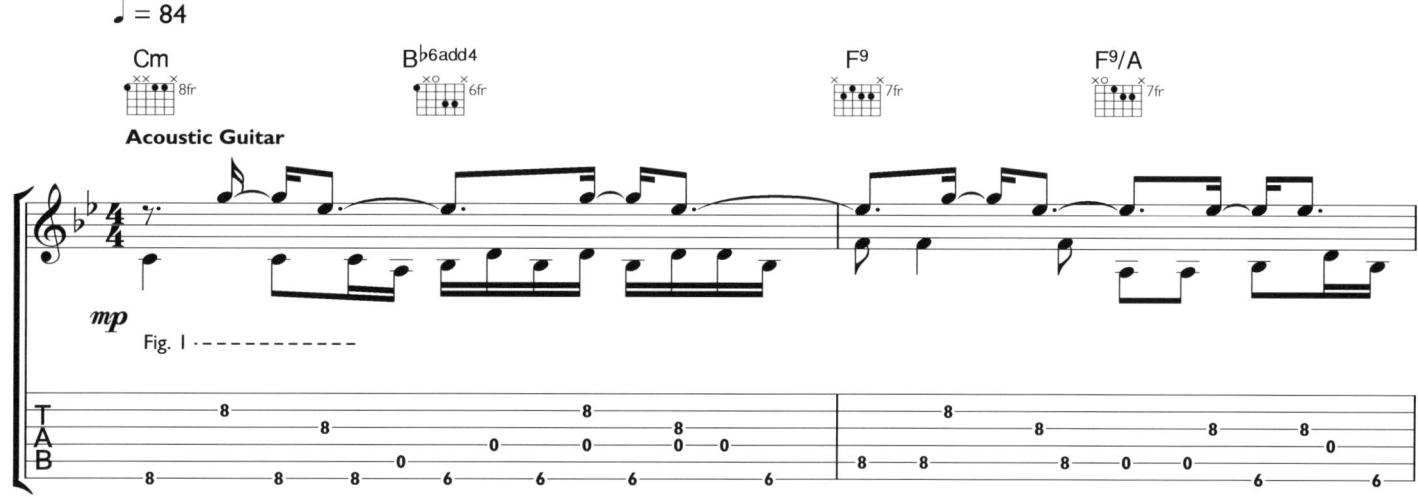

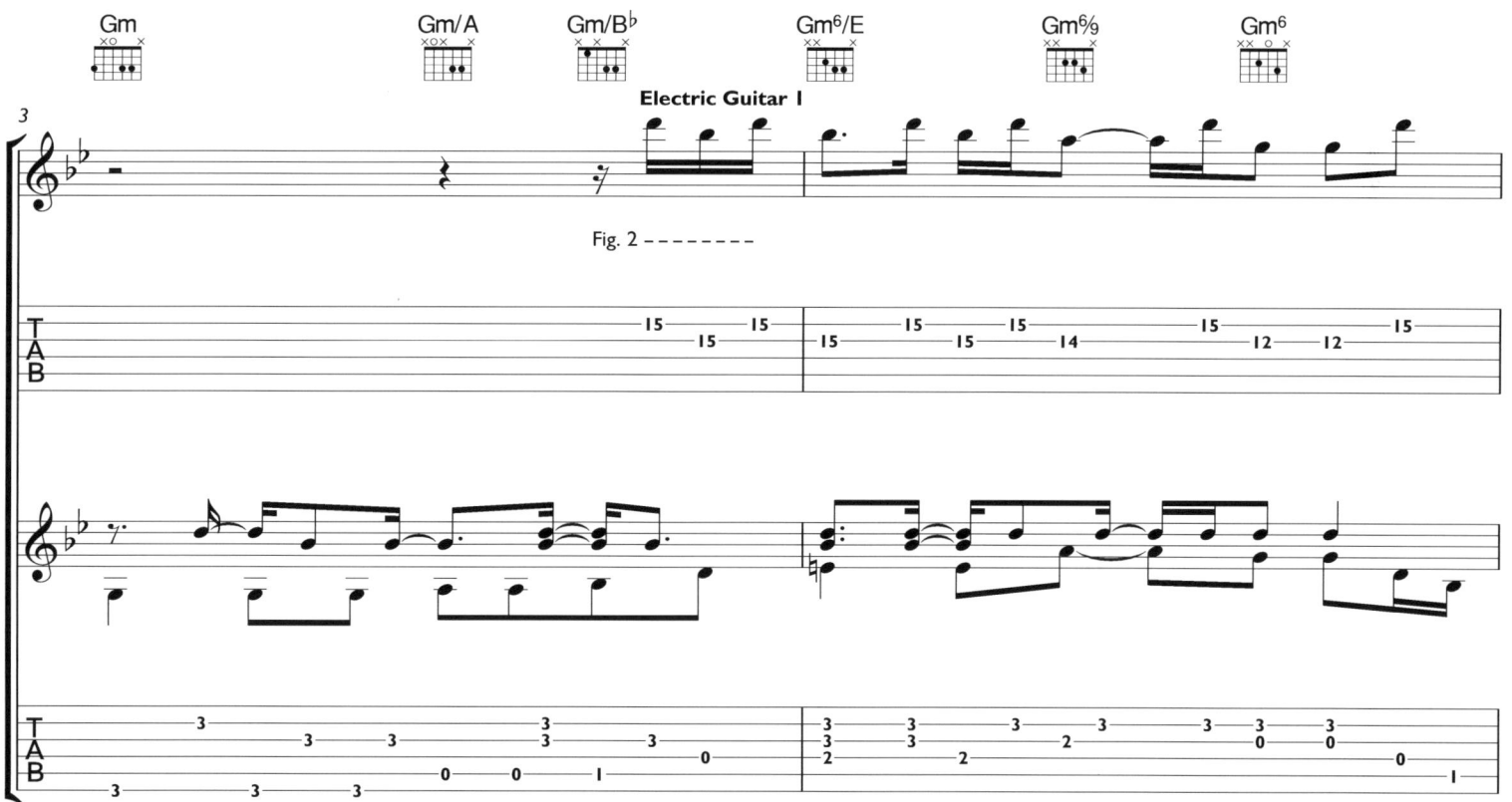

© 1997 Warner/Chappell Music Ltd
All Rights Reserved.

Gm6
Dm(add9)/F
E7
17
What's
that??
all.
Electric Guitar 1
mf
Acoustic Guitar

Gm6
Dm(add9)/F
E7
20
What's
that??

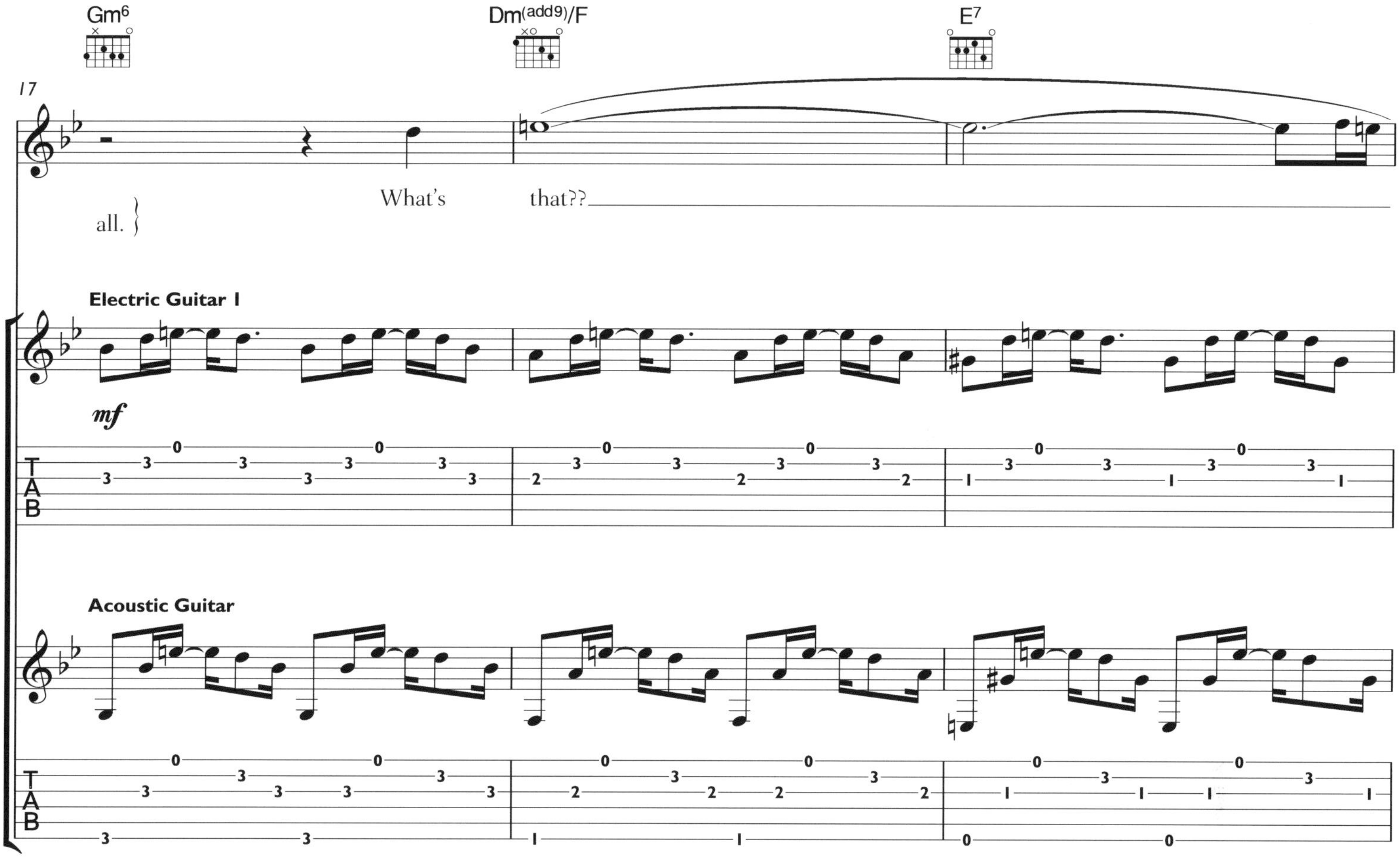

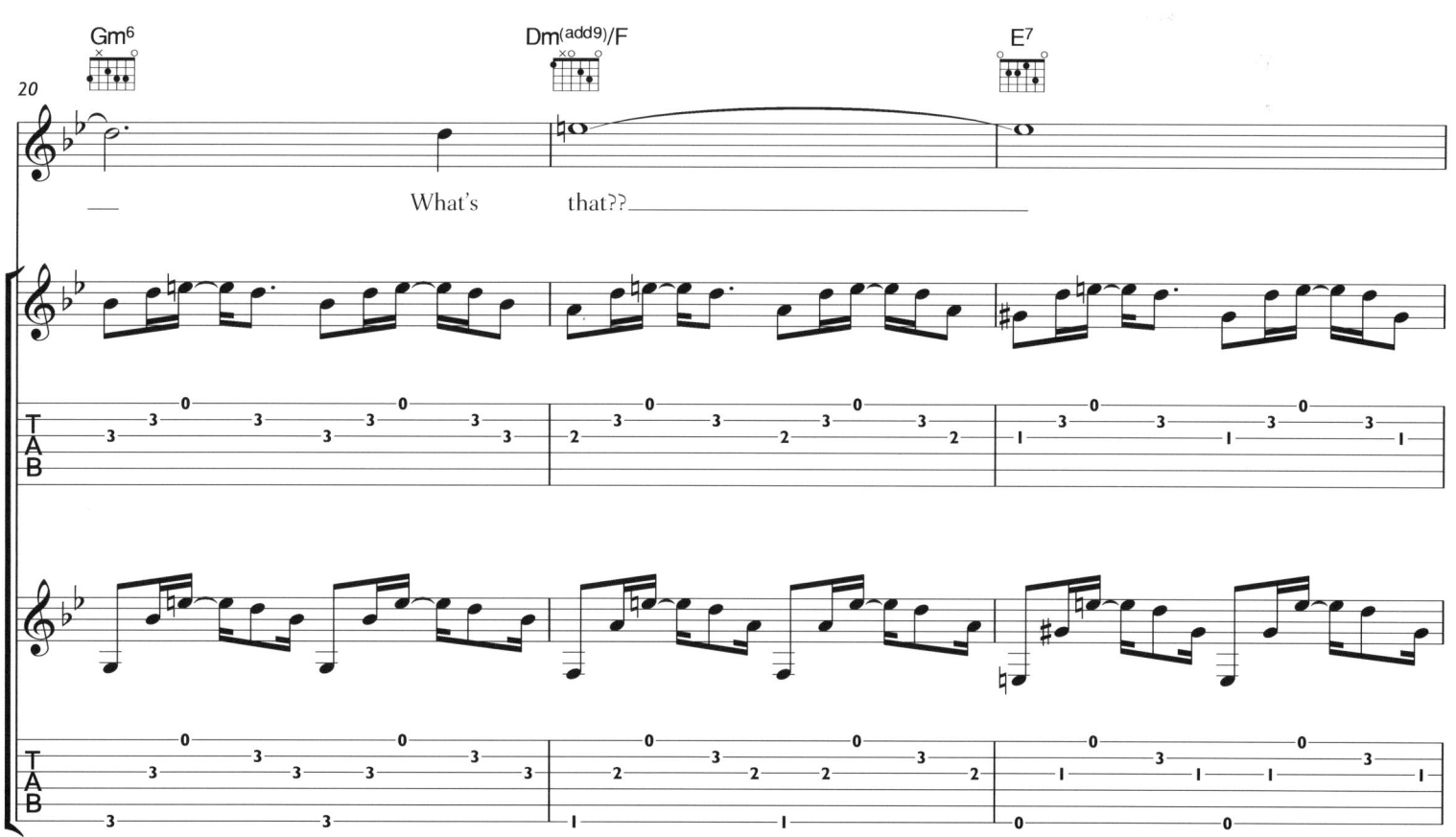

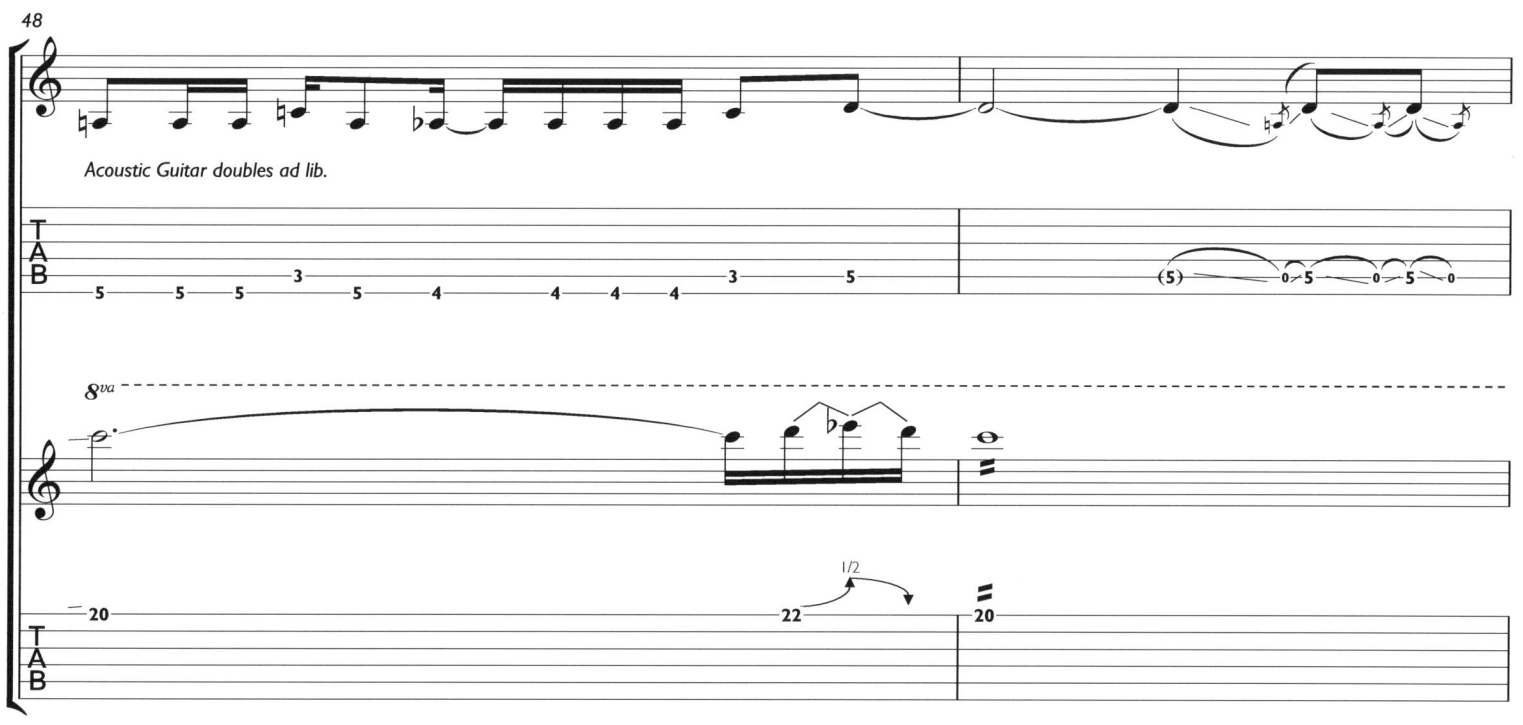

EXIT MUSIC (FOR A FILM)

Words and Music by Thomas Yorke, Jonathan Greenwood,
Colin Greenwood, Edward O'Brien and Philip Selway

© 1997 Warner/Chappell Music Ltd
All Rights Reserved.

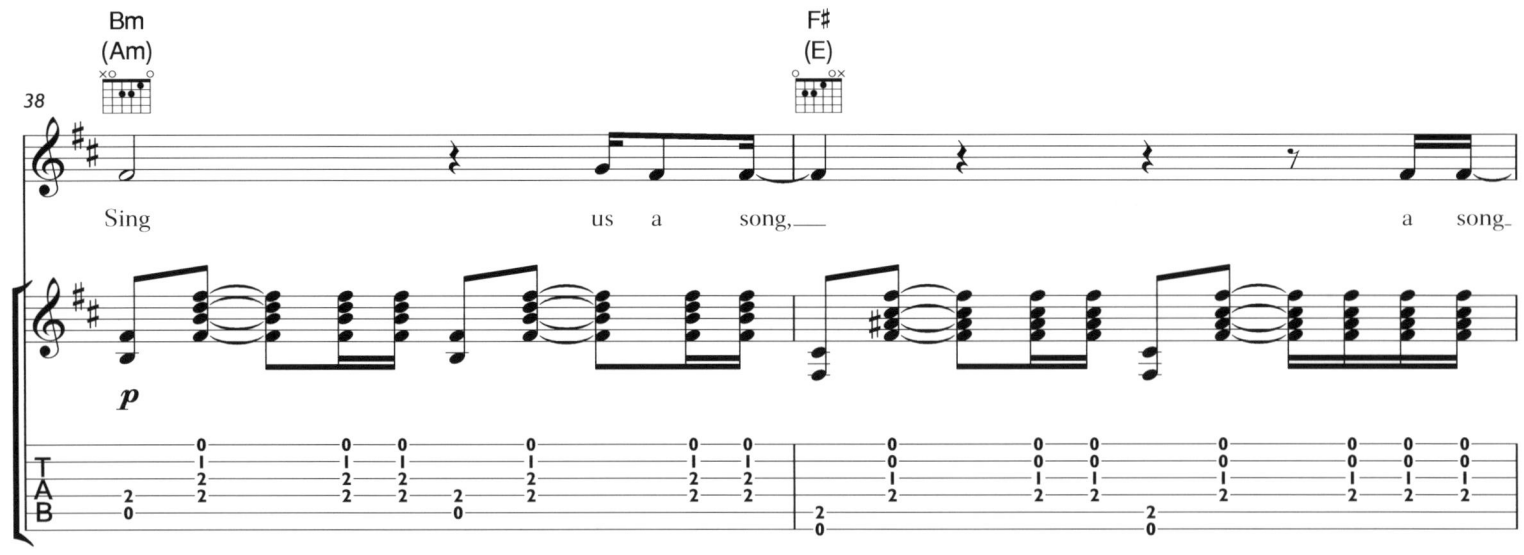
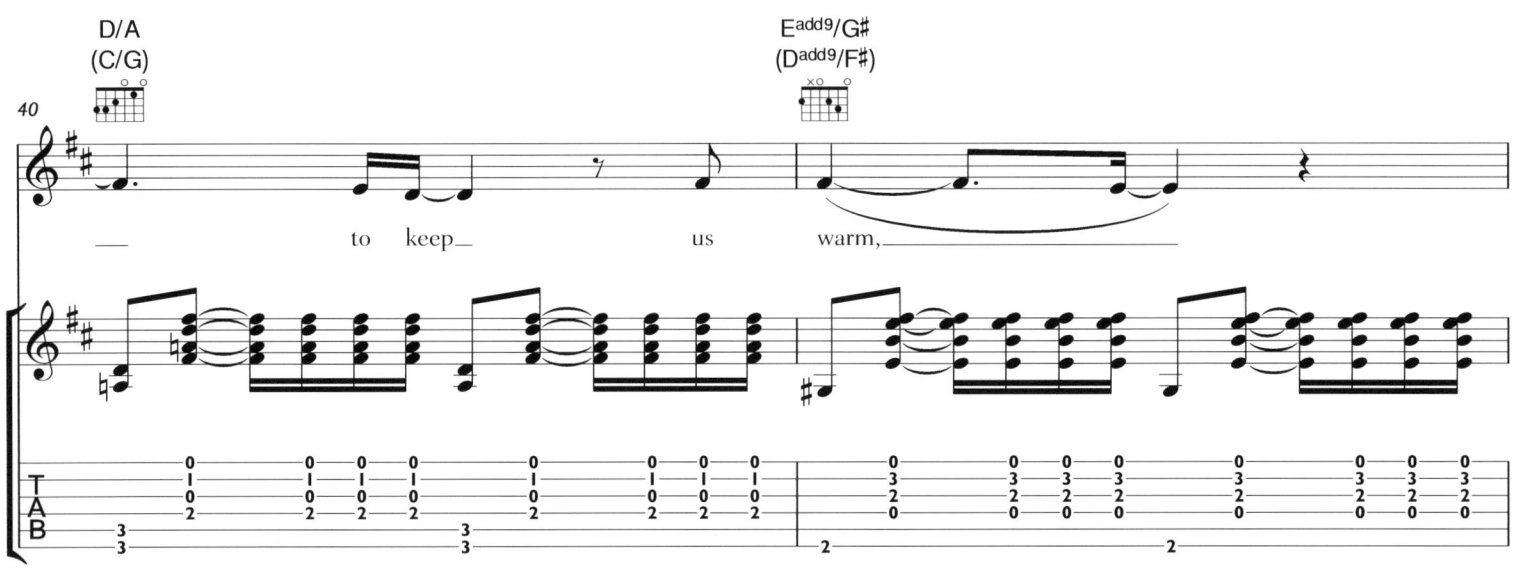

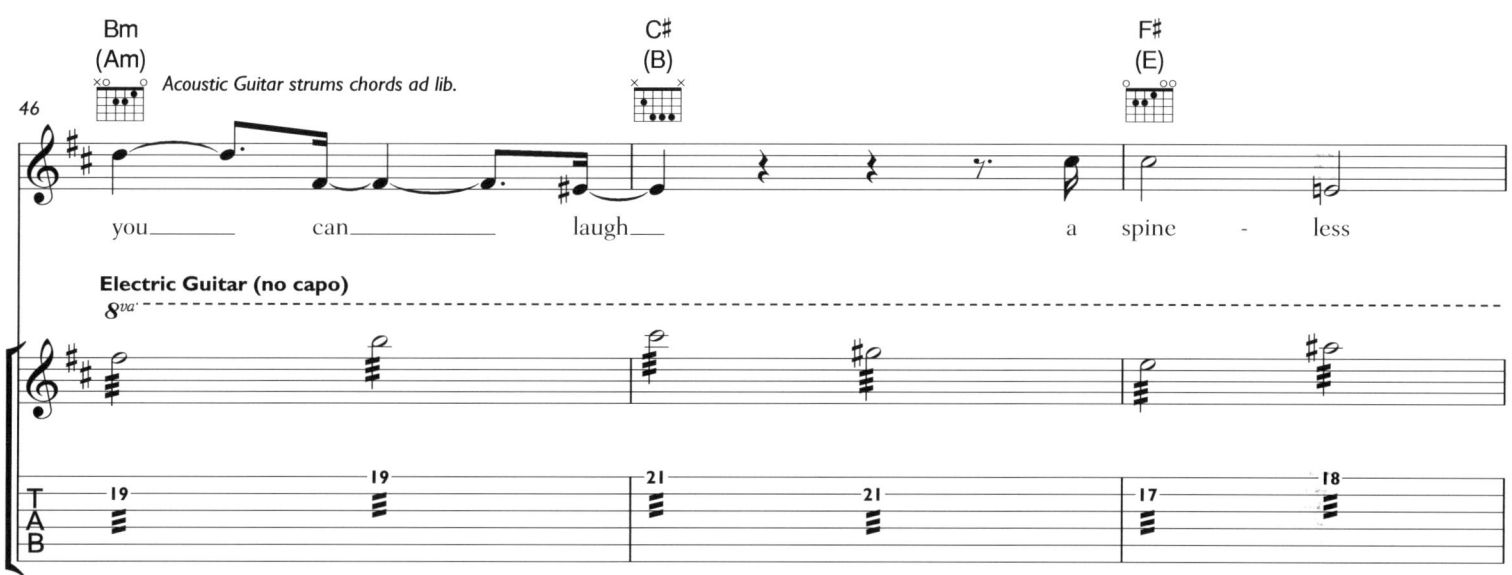
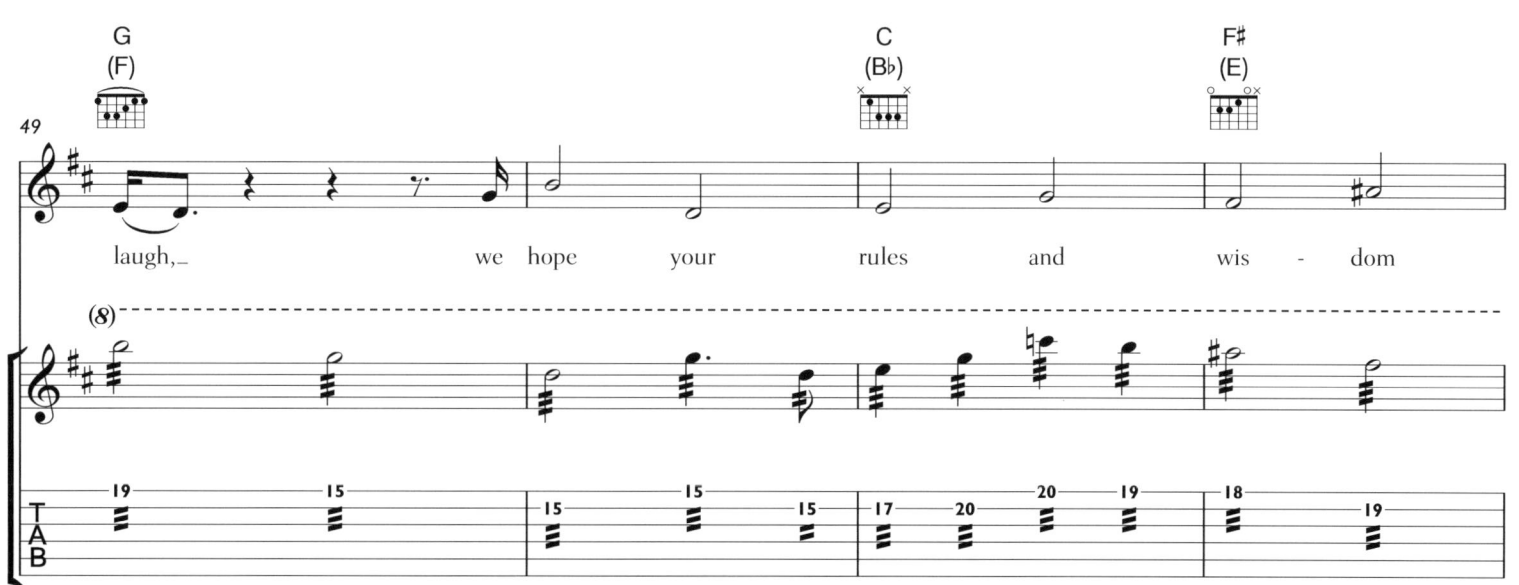

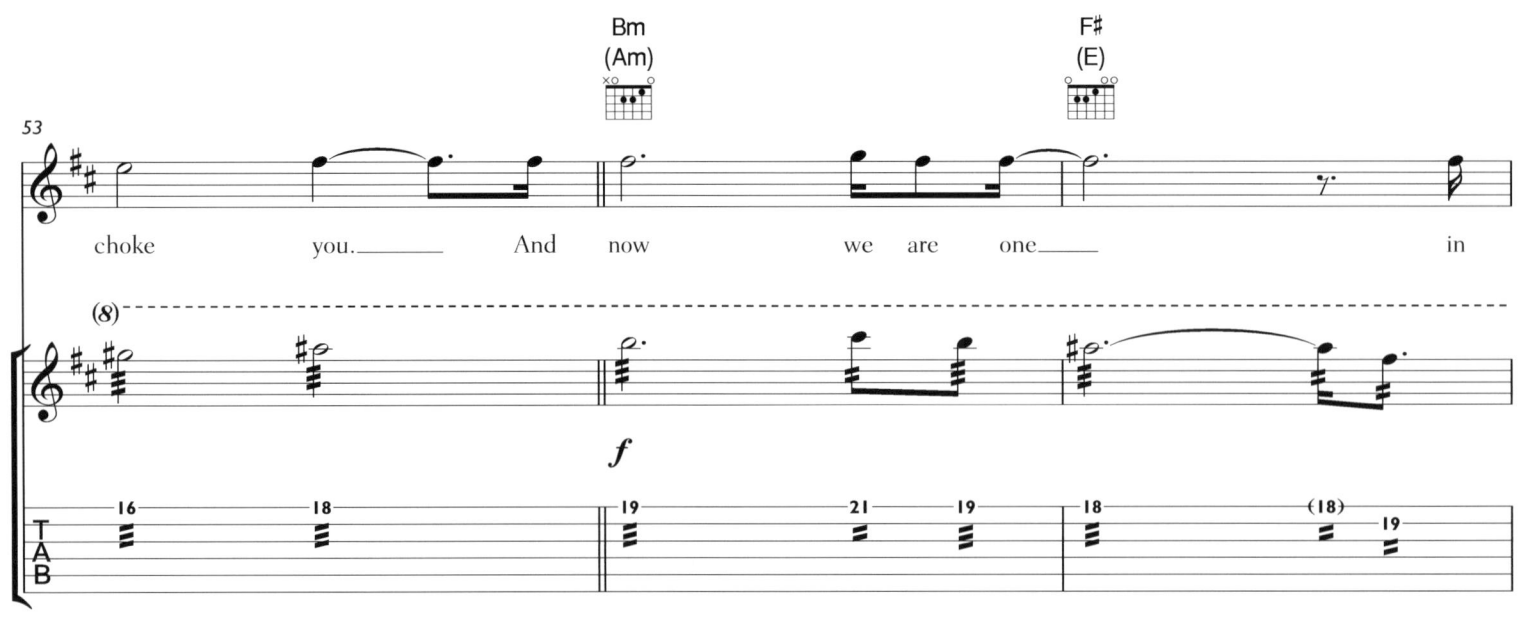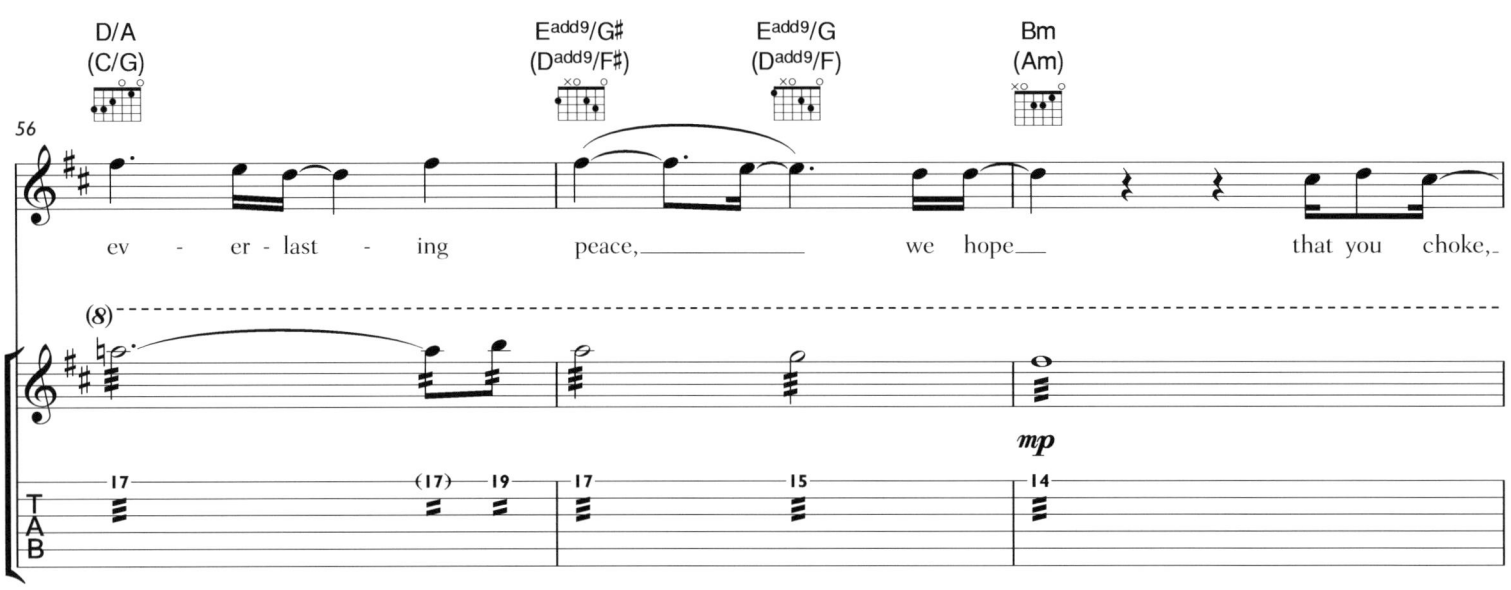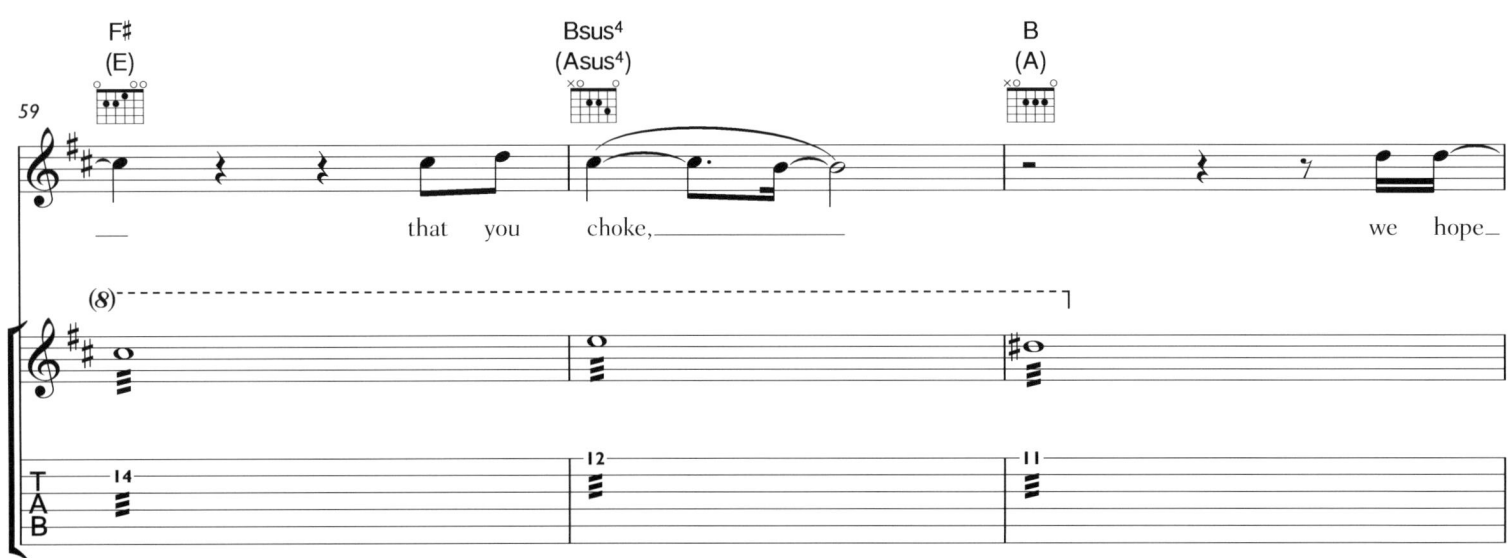

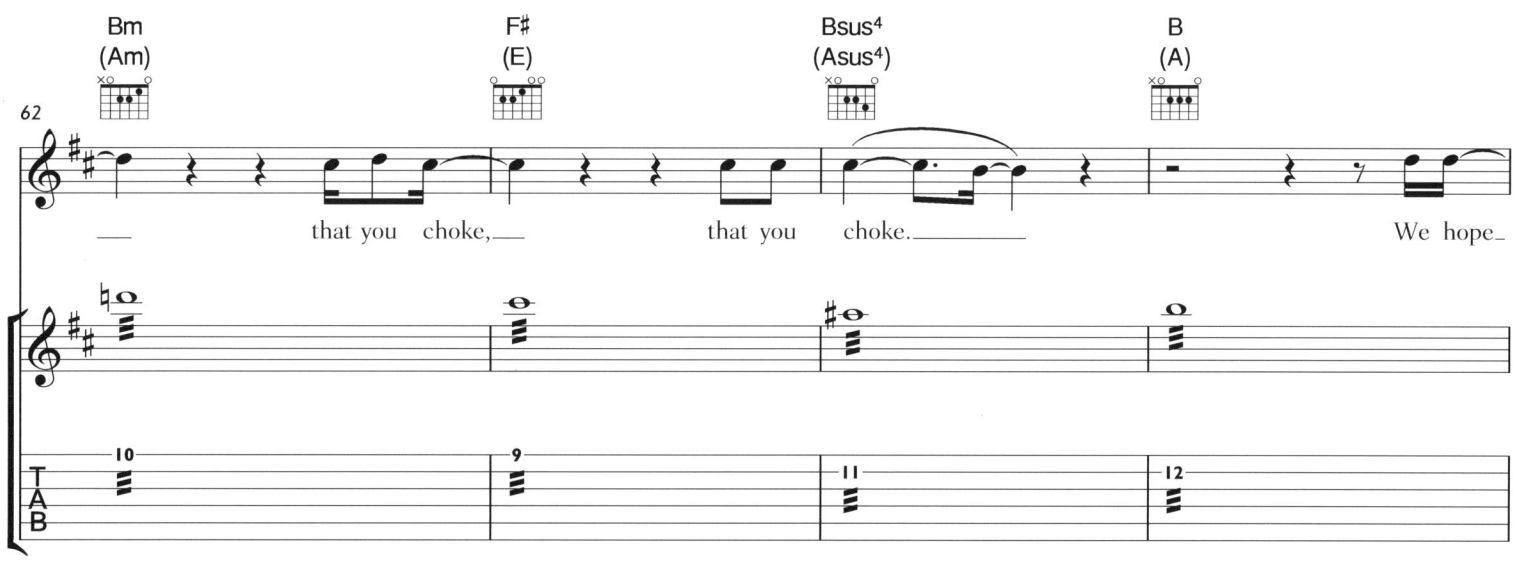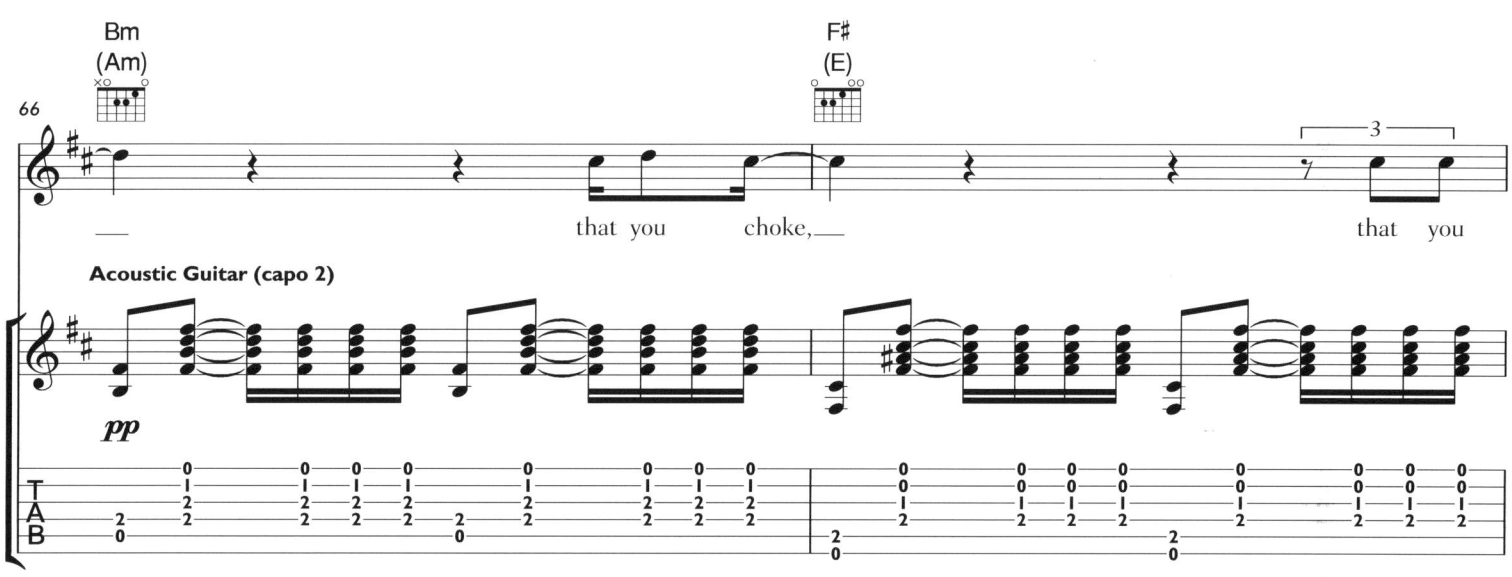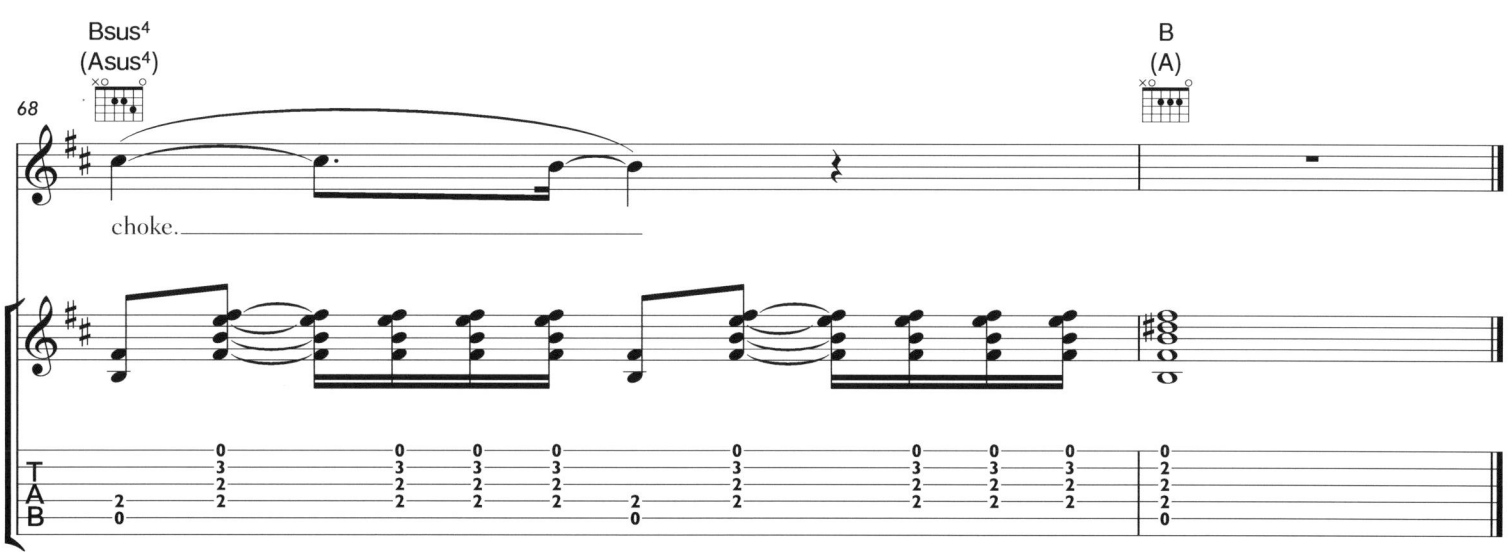

LET DOWN

Words and Music by Thomas Yorke, Jonathan Greenwood, Colin Greenwood, Edward O'Brien and Philip Selway

© 1997 Warner/Chappell Music Ltd
All Rights Reserved.

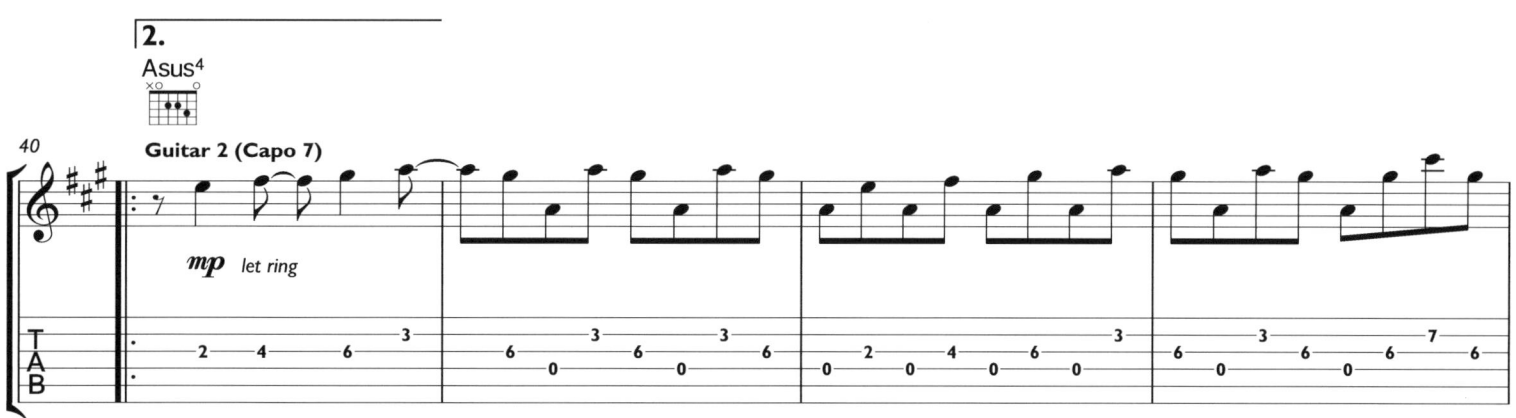
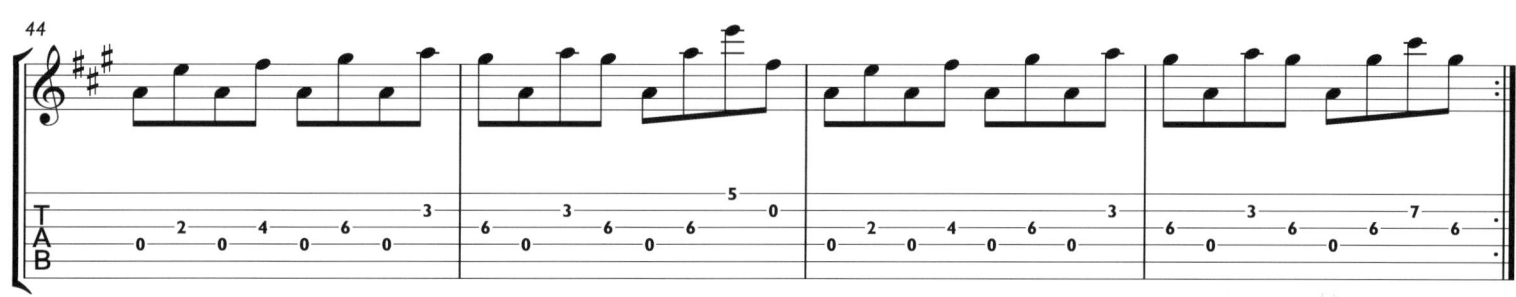
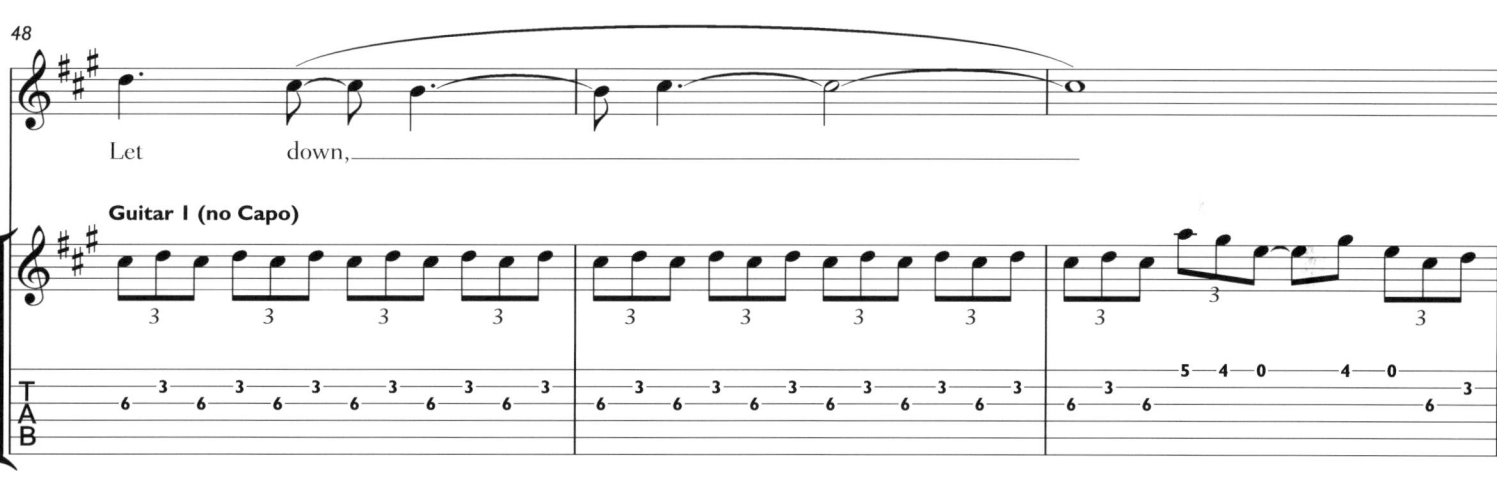

Let down,

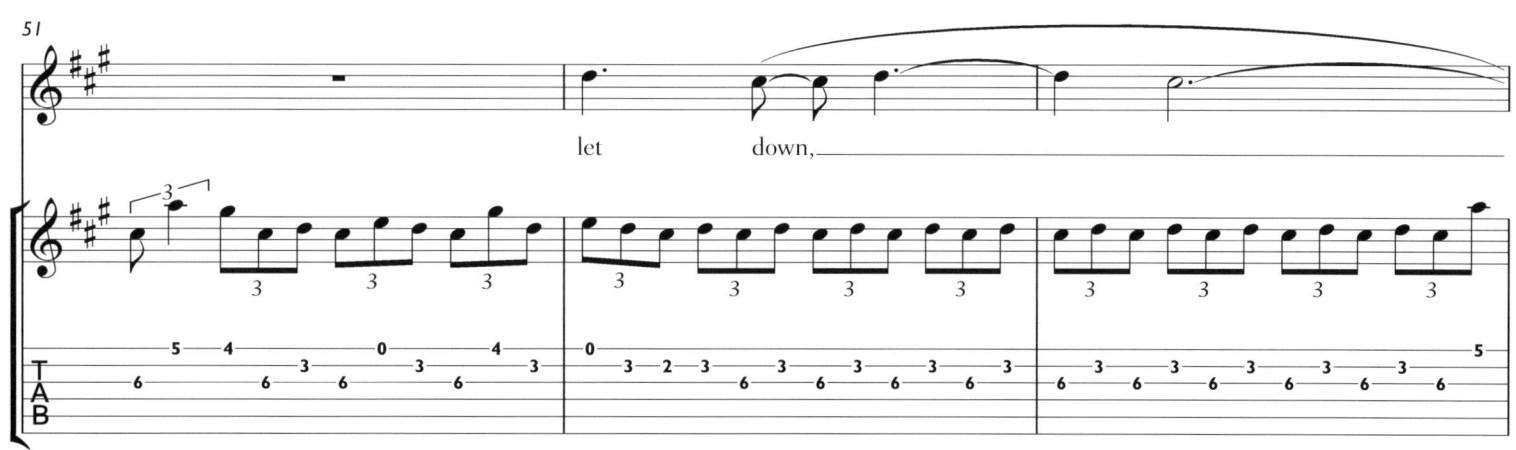

let down,

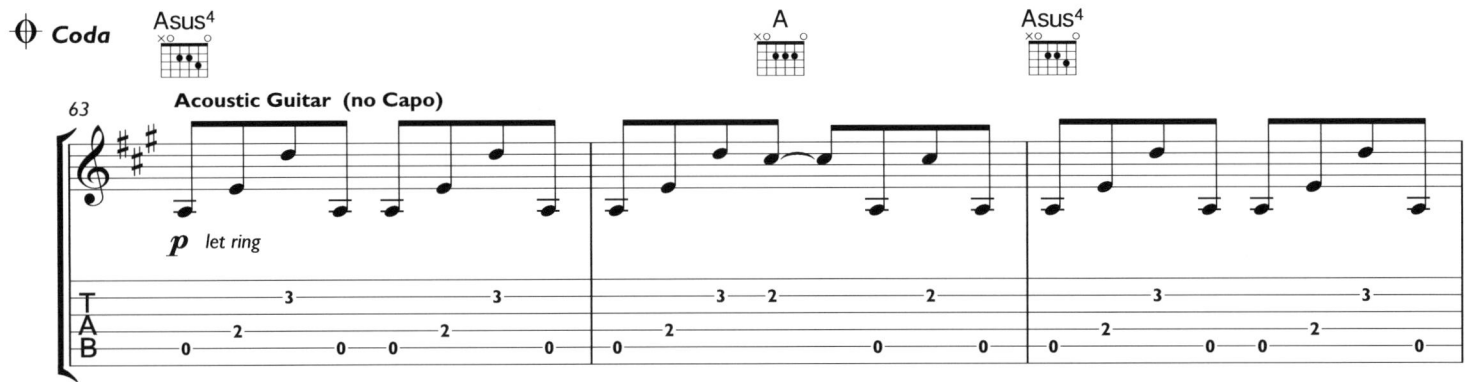
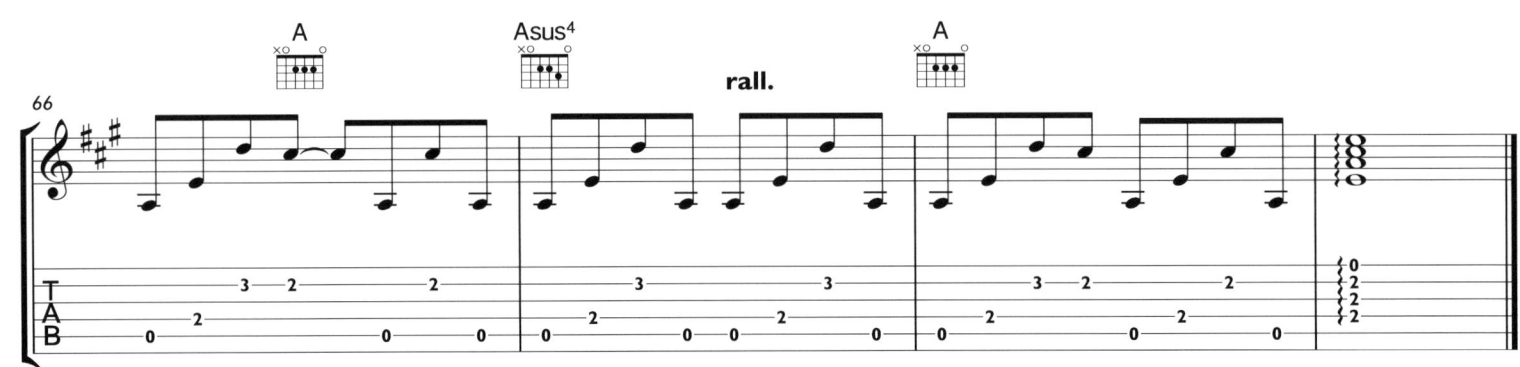

KARMA POLICE

Words and Music by Thomas Yorke, Jonathan Greenwood, Colin Greenwood, Edward O'Brien and Philip Selway

© 1997 Warner/Chappell Music Ltd
All Rights Reserved.

46

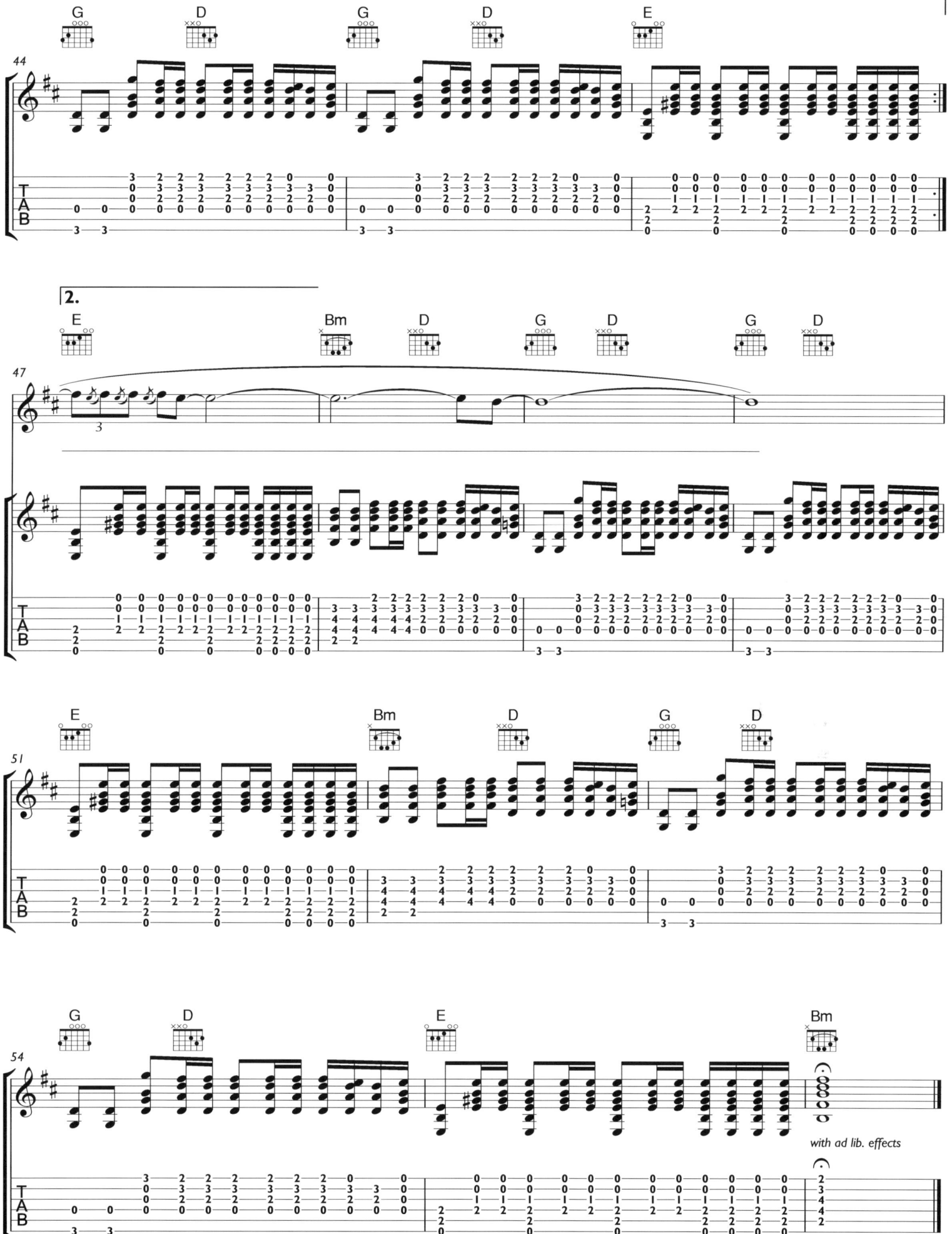

fitter happier

Words and Music by Thomas Yorke, Jonathan Greenwood, Colin Greenwood, Edward O'Brien and Philip Selway

♩ = 76 **Freely**

Fitter, happier, more productive, comfortable, not drinking too much,
regular exercise at the gym (3 days a week), getting on better with your associate
employee contemporaries, at ease, eating well (no more microwave dinners and saturated fats),

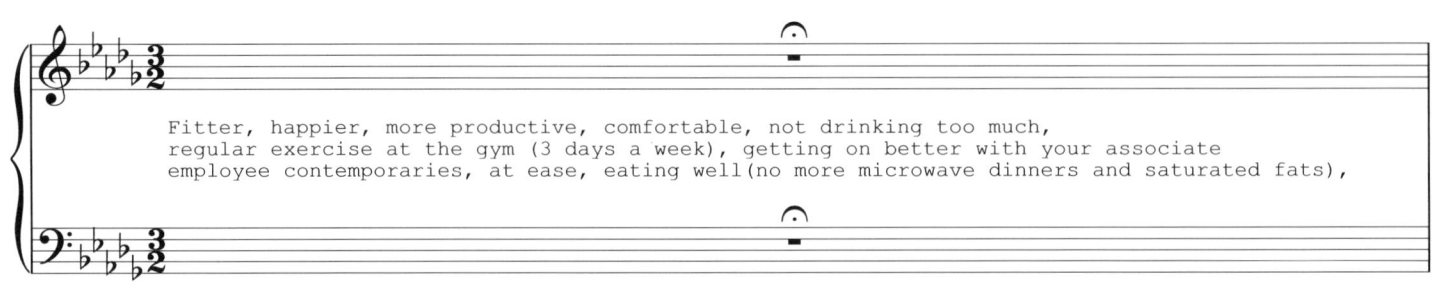

a patient better driver, a safer car (baby smiling in back seat), sleeping well (no bad dreams),
no paranoia, careful to all animals (never washing spiders down the plughole),

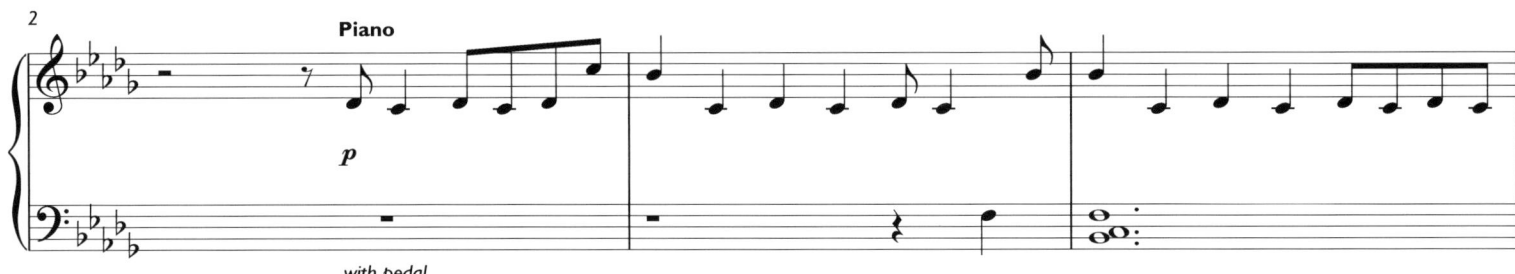

keep in contact with old friends (enjoy a drink now and then), will frequently check credit at
(moral) bank (hole in wall), favours for favours, fond but not in love, charity standing orders,

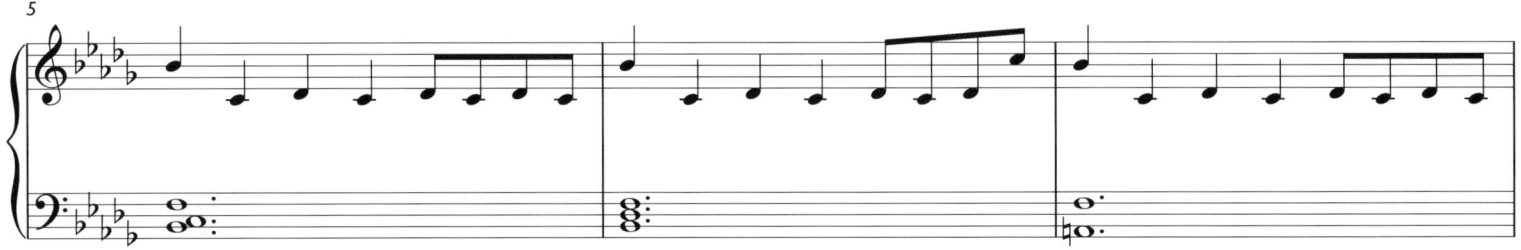

© 1997 Warner/Chappell Music Ltd
All Rights Reserved.

on Sundays ring road supermarket (no killing moths or putting boiling water on the ants),
car wash (also on Sundays), no longer afraid of the dark or midday shadows,
nothing so ridiculously teenage and desperate,

nothing so childish, at a better pace, slower and more calculated, no chance of escape, now self-employed,
concerned (but powerless), an empowered & informed member of society (pragmatism not idealism),

will not cry in public, less chance of illness, tyres that grip in the wet
(shot of baby strapped in back seat), a good memory, still cries at a good film,

still kisses with saliva, no longer empty and frantic like a cat tied to a stick,
that's driven into frozen winter shit (the ability to laugh at weakness),
calm, fitter, healthier and more productive, a pig in a cage on antibiotics.

ELECTIONEERING

**Words and Music by Thomas Yorke, Jonathan Greenwood,
Colin Greenwood, Edward O'Brien and Philip Selway**

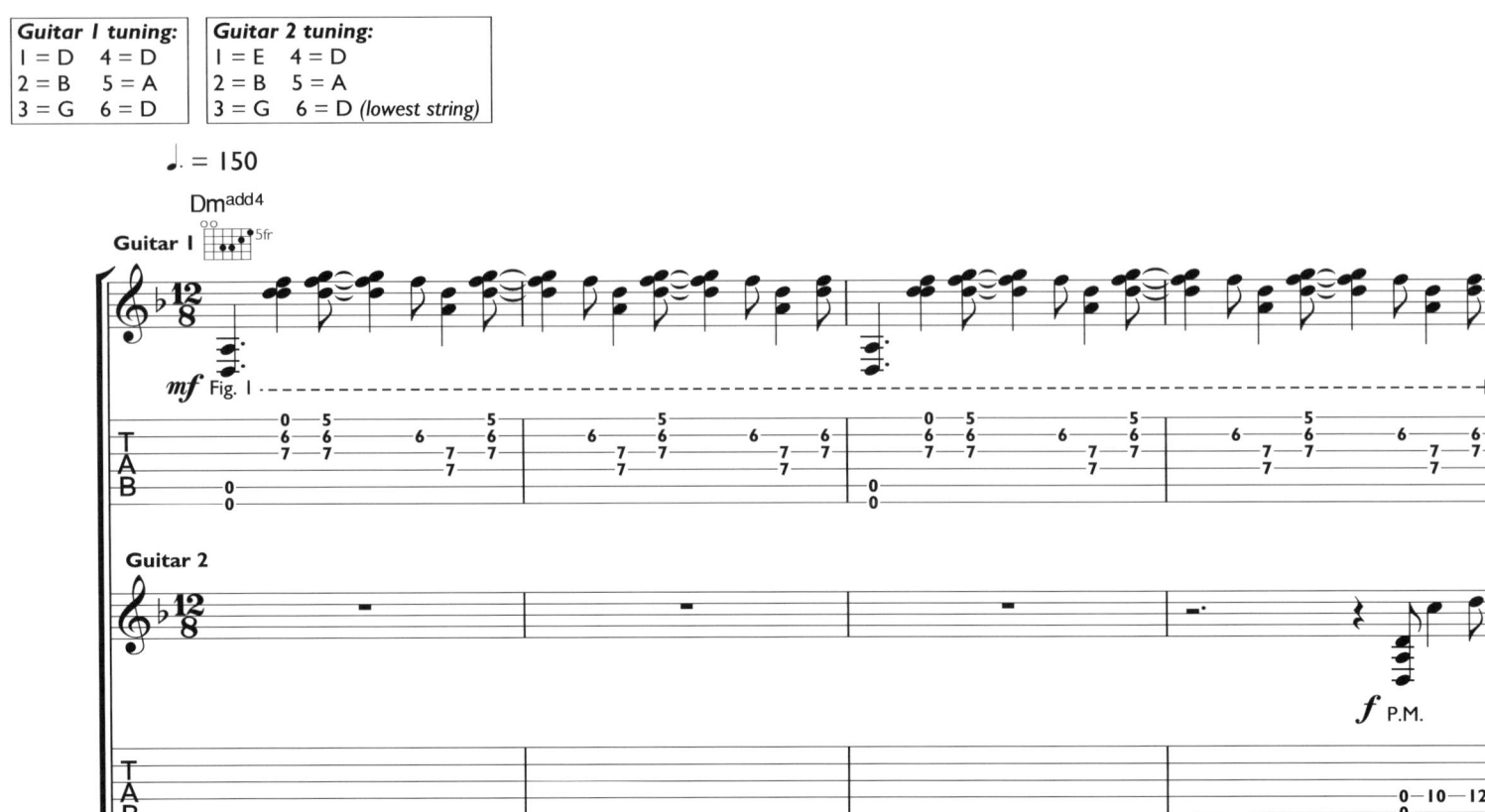

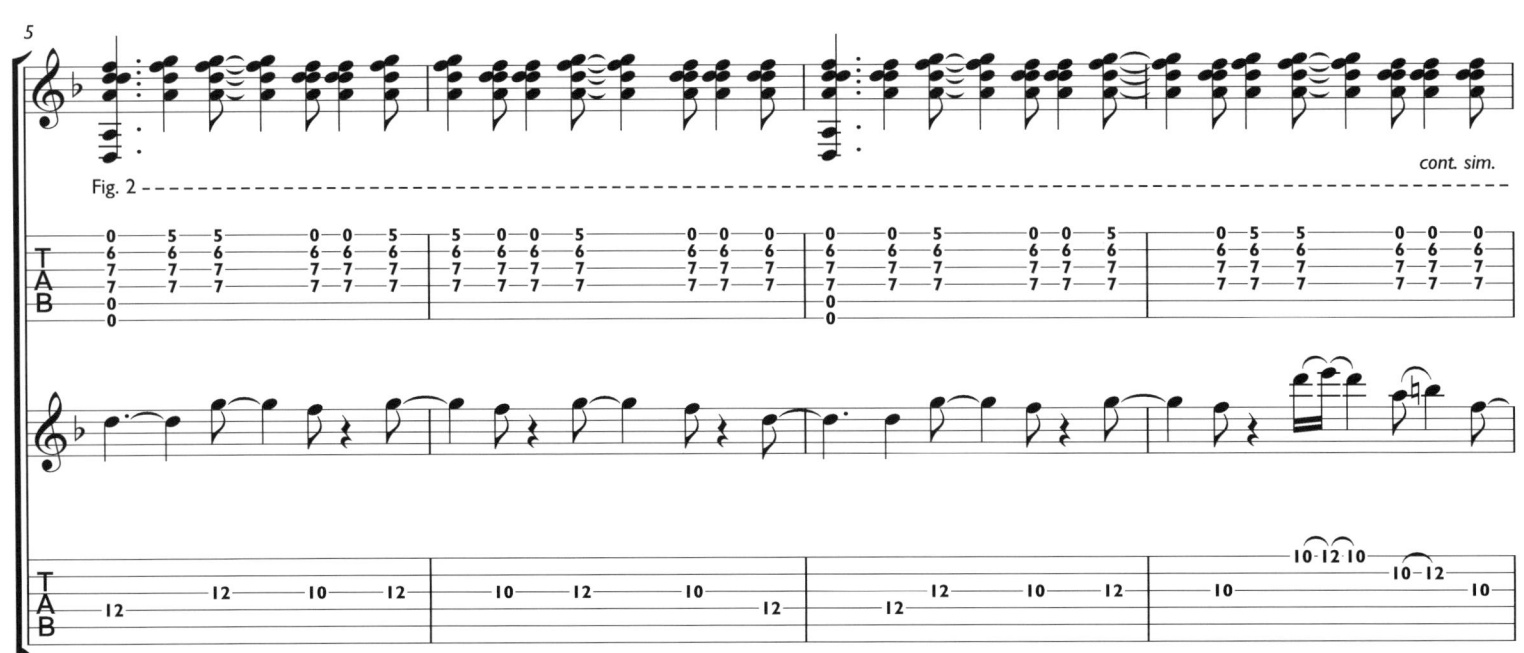

© 1997 Warner/Chappell Music Ltd
All Rights Reserved.

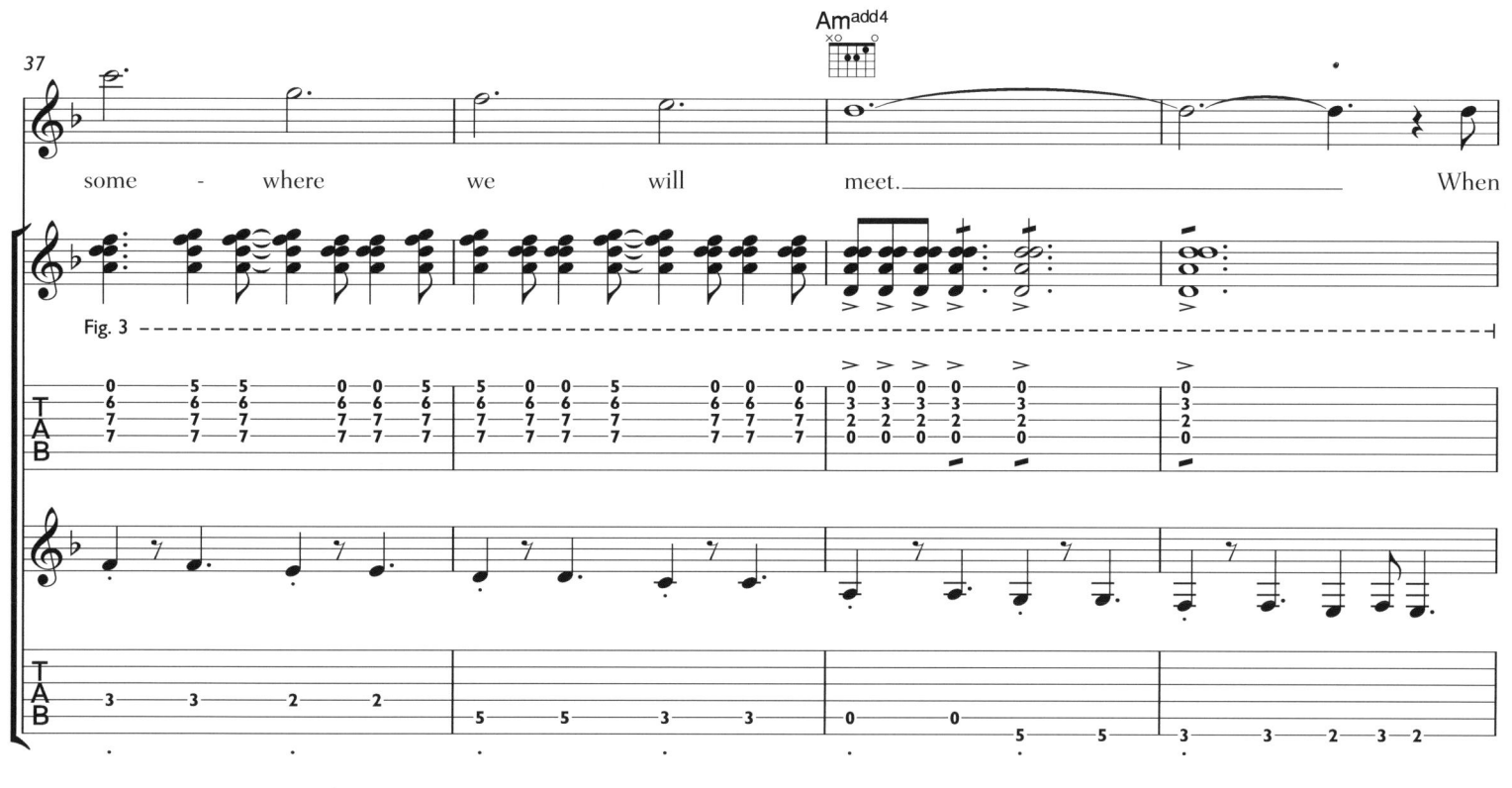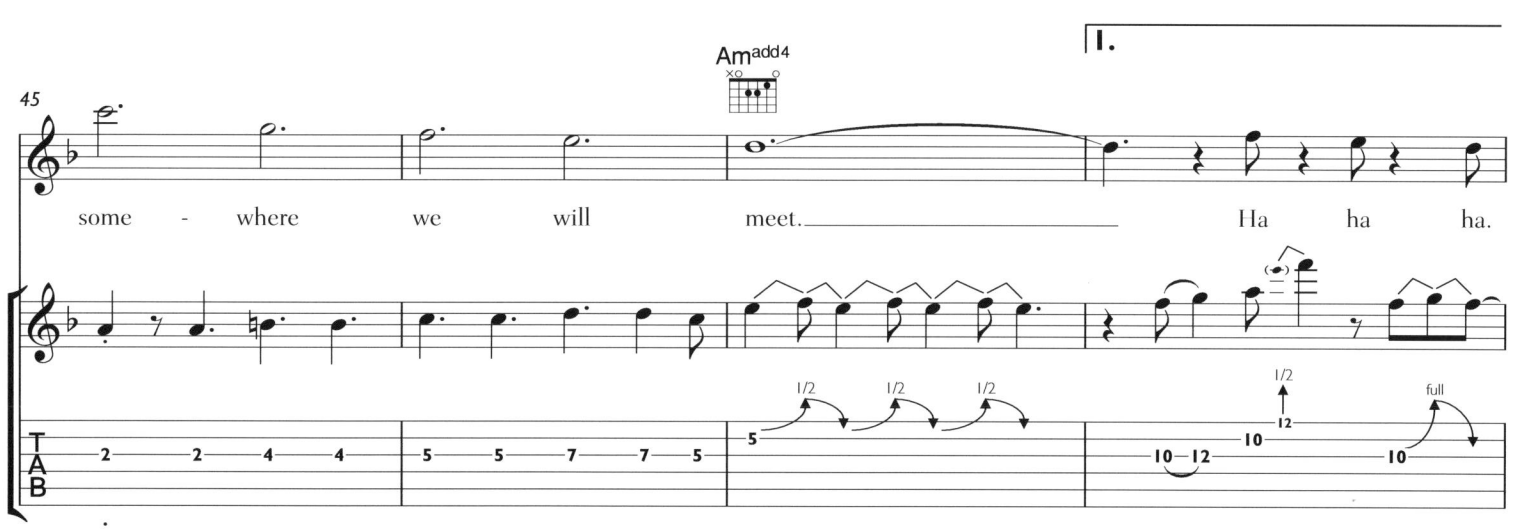

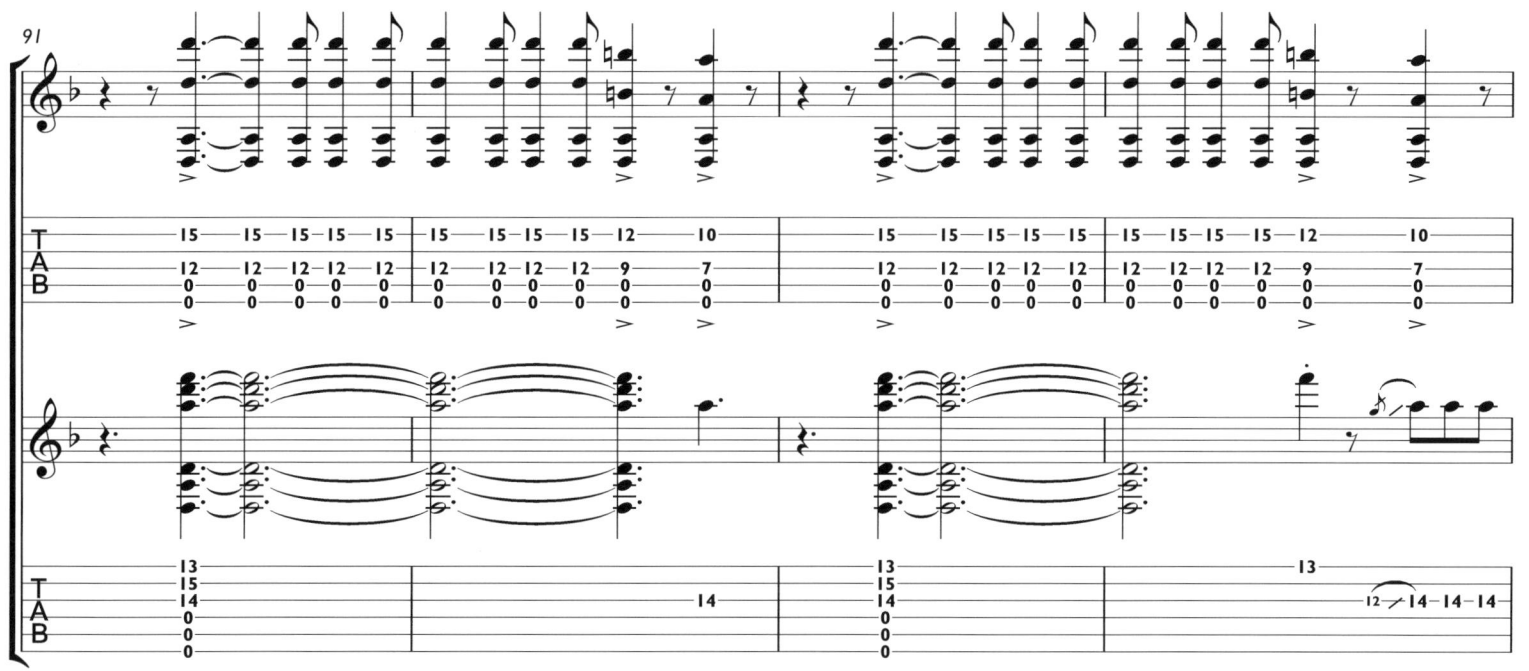
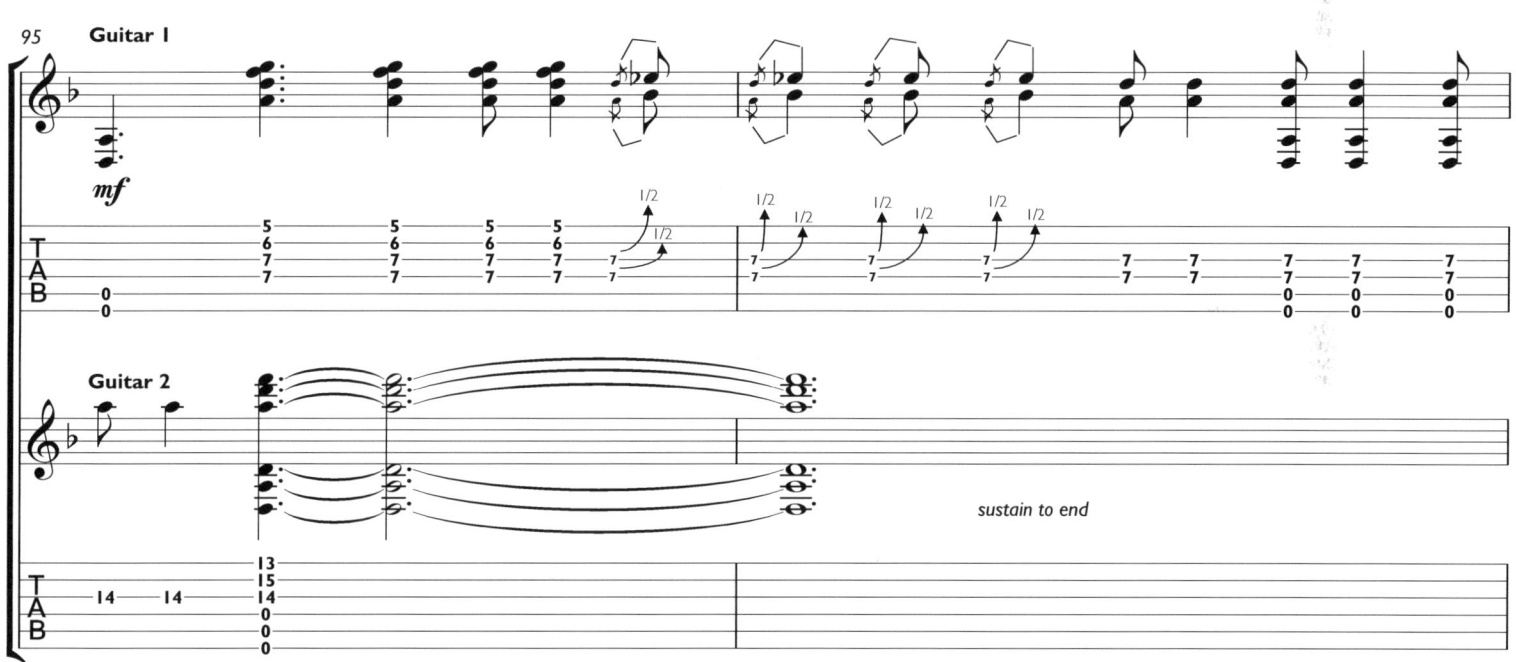
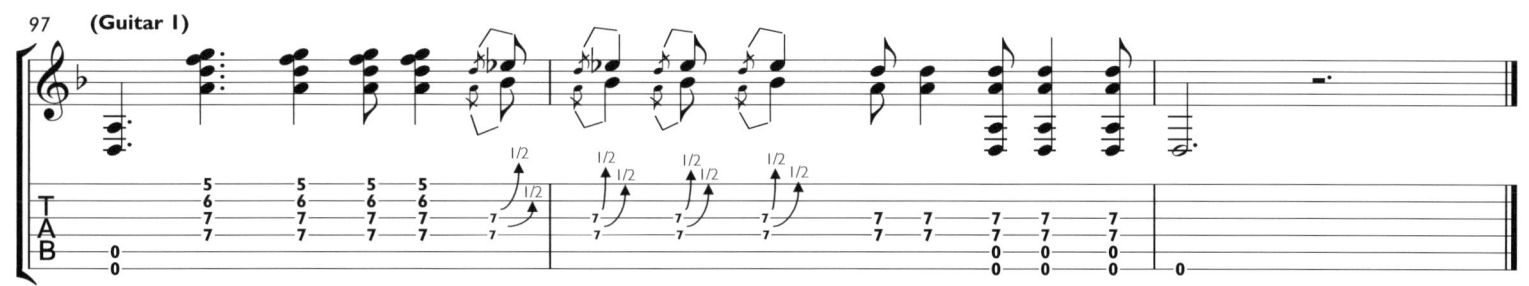

CLIMBING UP THE WALLS

*Words and Music by Thomas Yorke, Jonathan Greenwood,
Colin Greenwood, Edward O'Brien and Philip Selway*

© 1997 Warner/Chappell Music Ltd
All Rights Reserved.

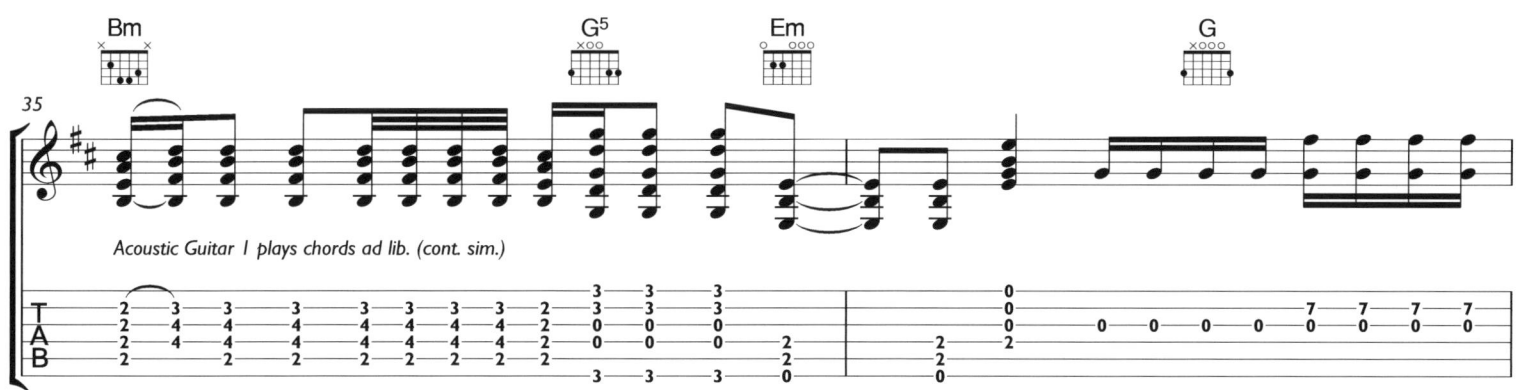
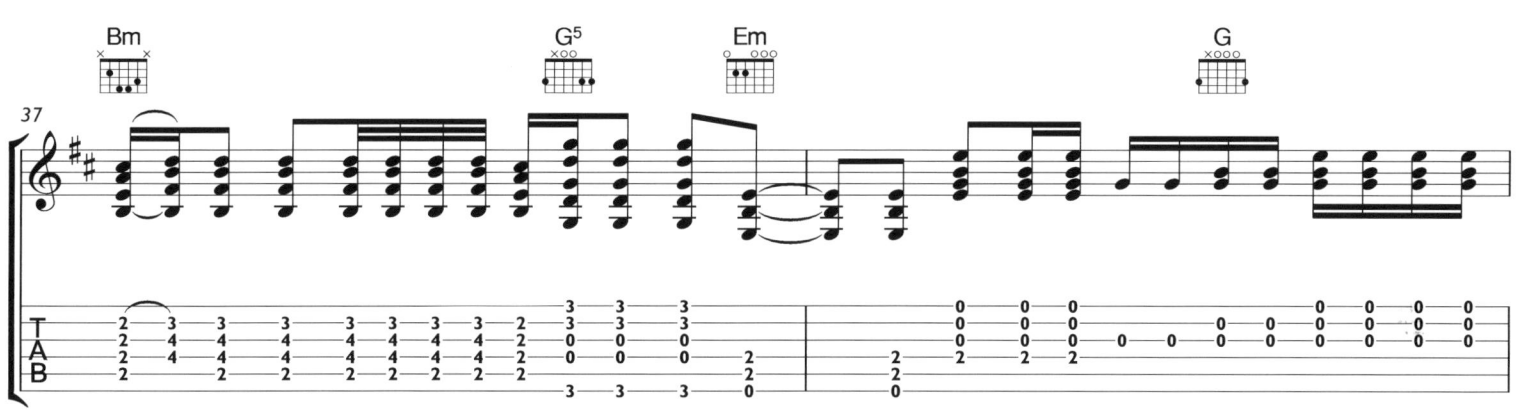
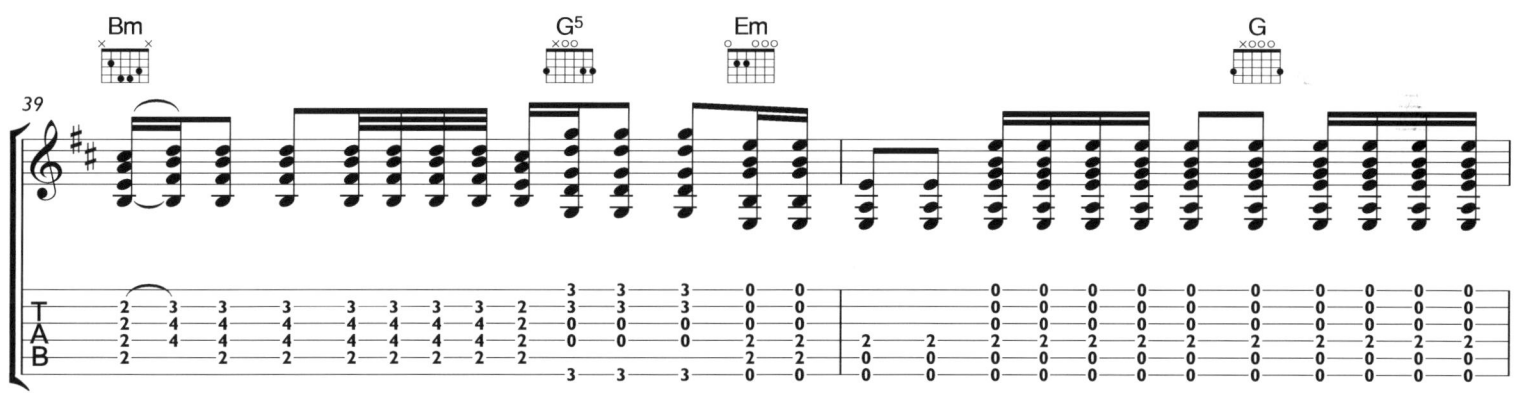
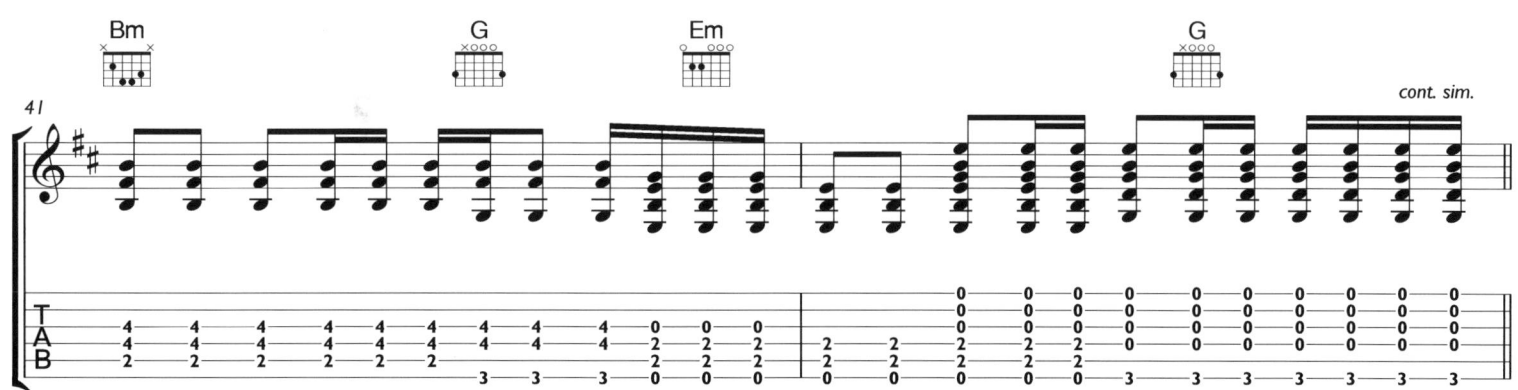

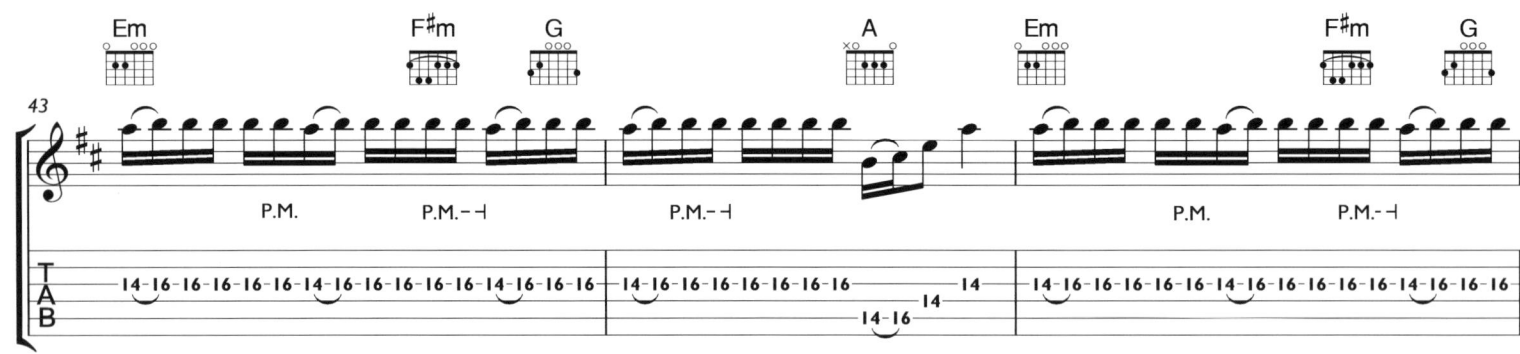
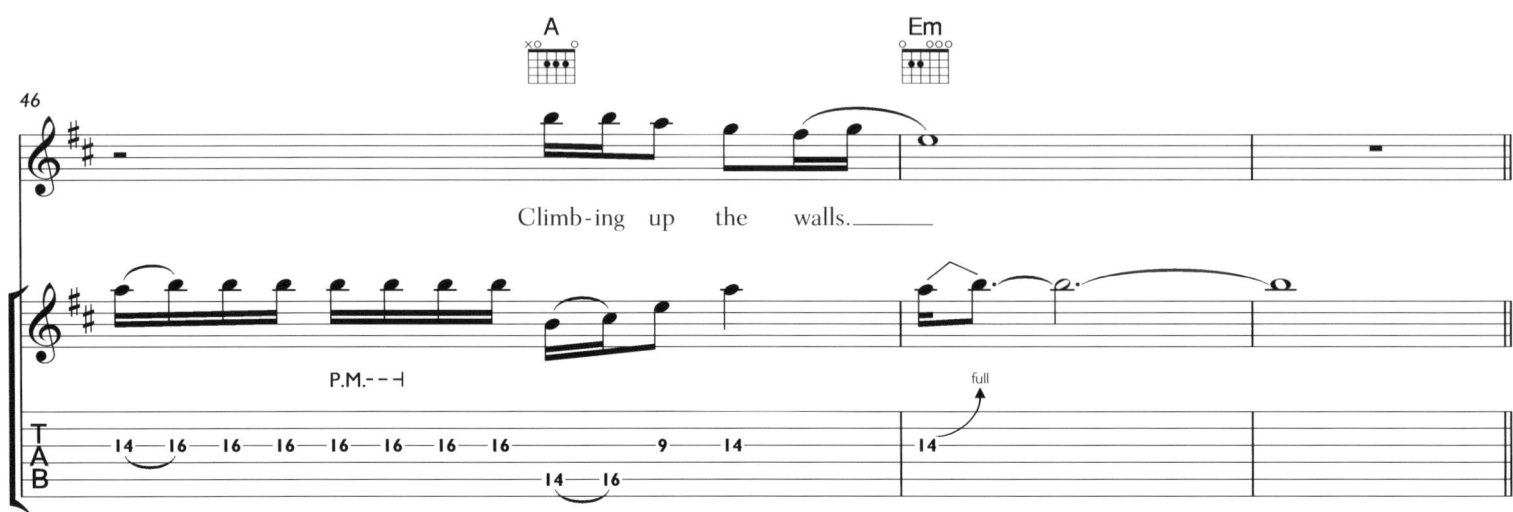
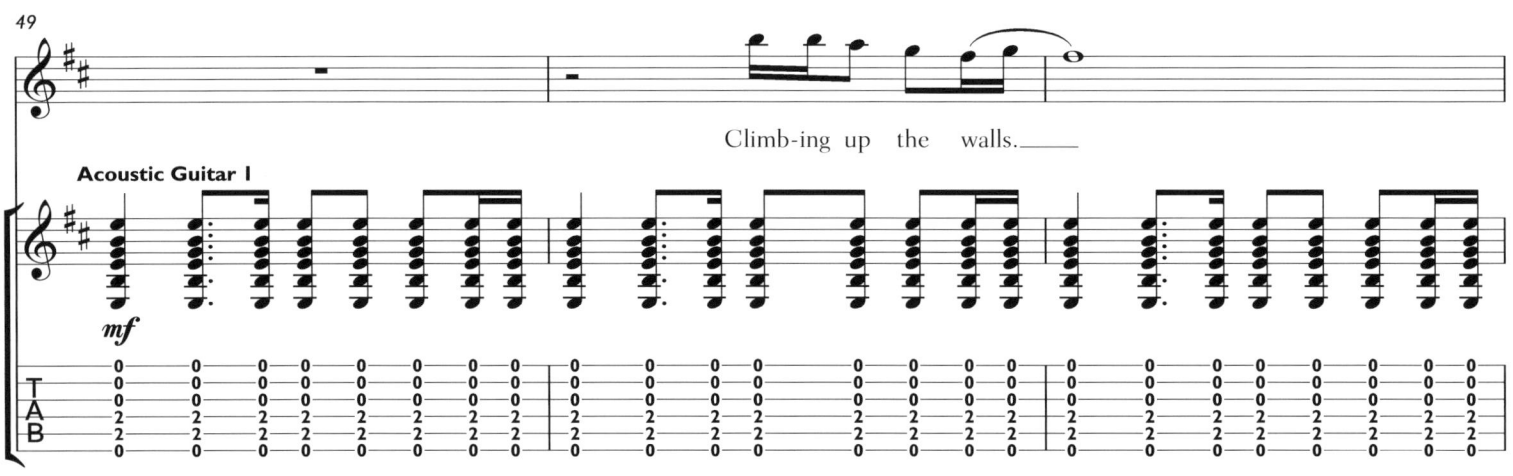
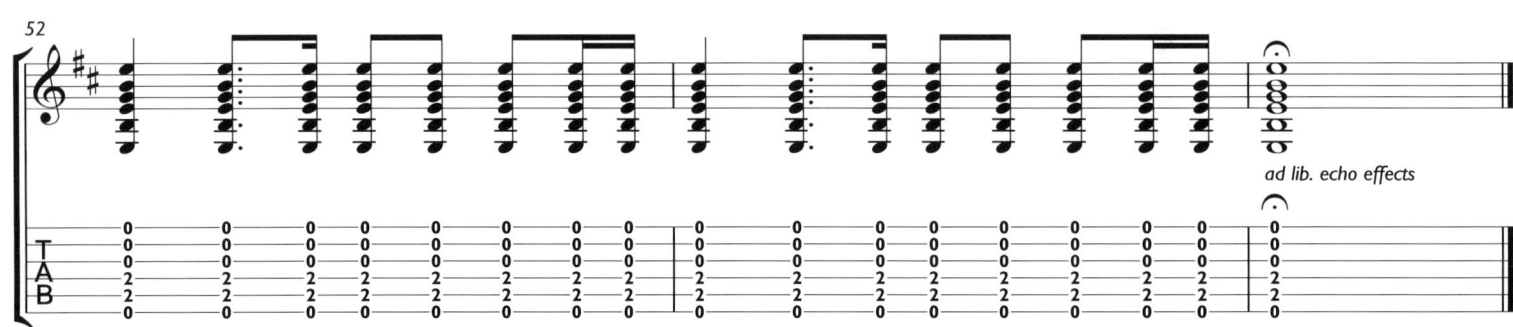

NO SURPRISES

Words and Music by Thomas Yorke, Jonathan Greenwood,
Colin Greenwood, Edward O'Brien and Philip Selway

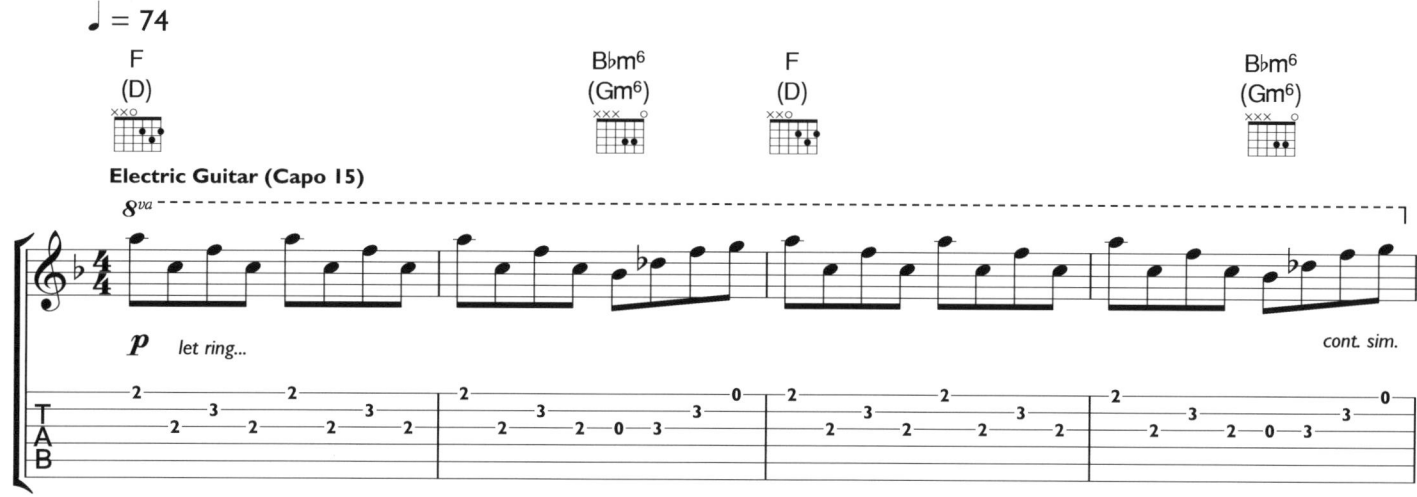
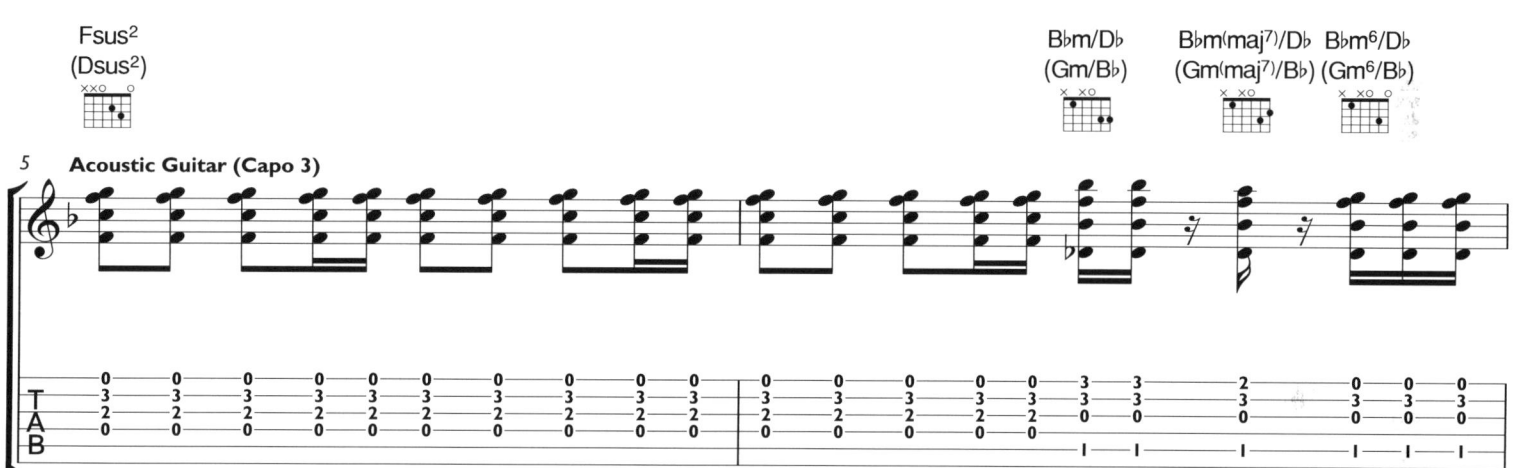
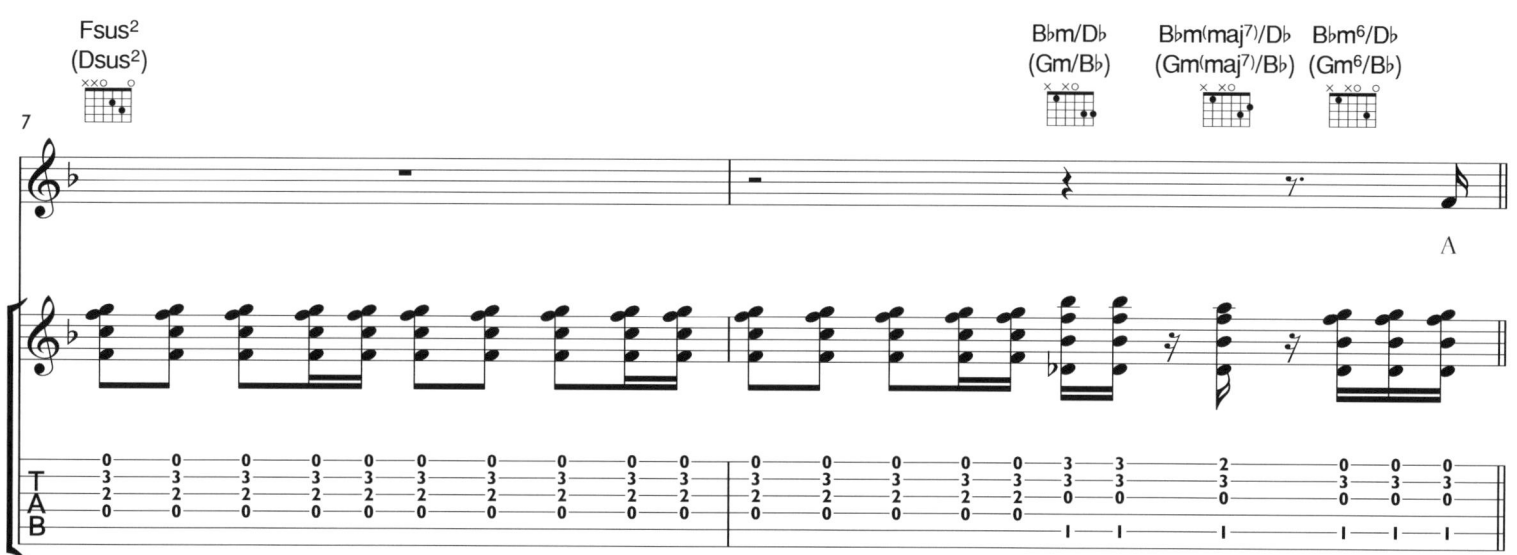

© 1997 Warner/Chappell Music Ltd
All Rights Reserved.

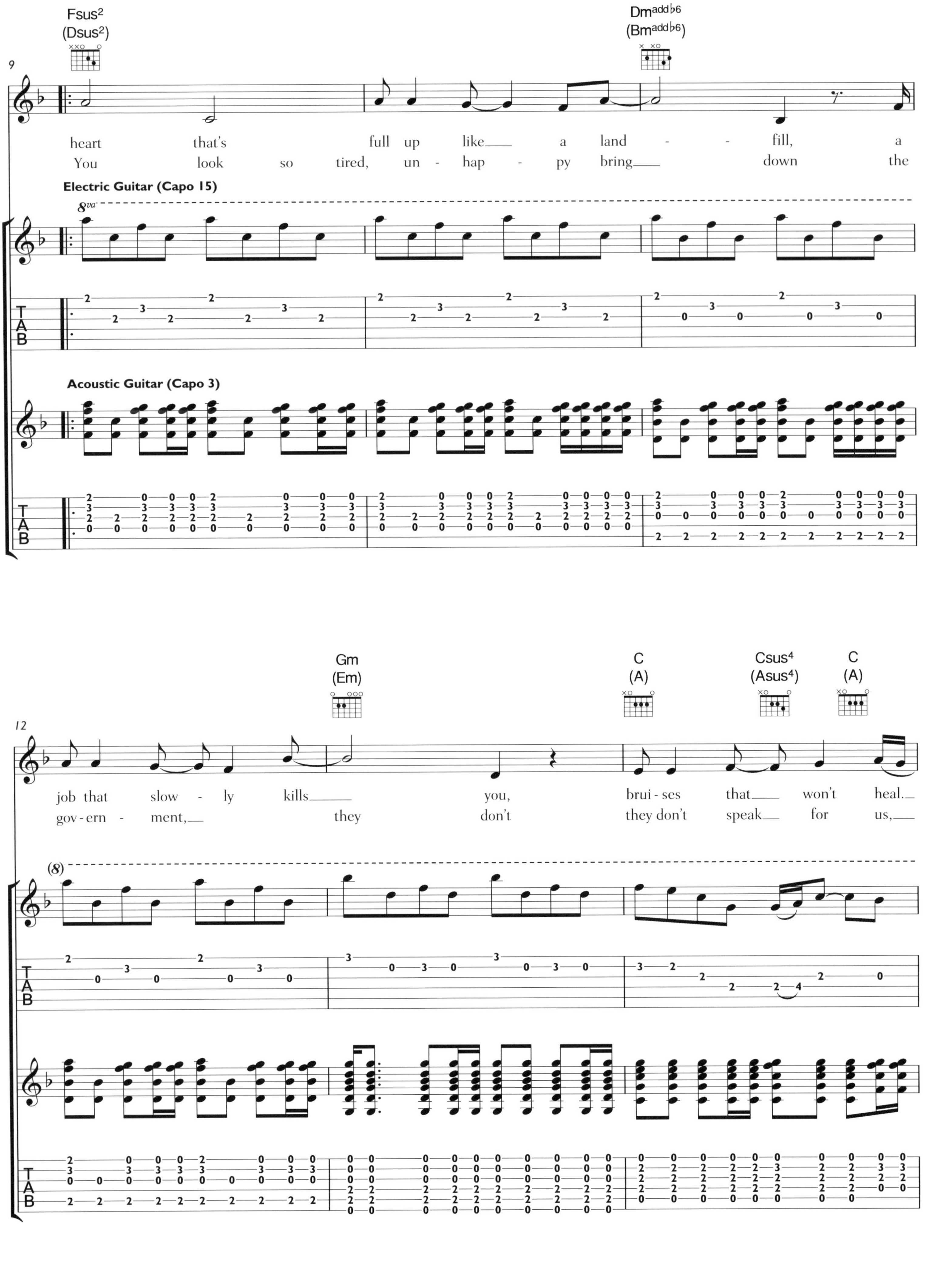
Fsus2 (Dsus2)
Dmadd♭6 (Bmadd♭6)
9
heart that's full up like a land - - fill, a
You look so tired, un - hap - py bring down the
Electric Guitar (Capo 15)
8va
Acoustic Guitar (Capo 3)
Gm (Em)
C (A)
Csus4 (Asus4)
C (A)
12
job that slow - ly kills you,
gov - ern - ment, they don't
brui - ses that won't heal.
they don't speak for us,
(8)

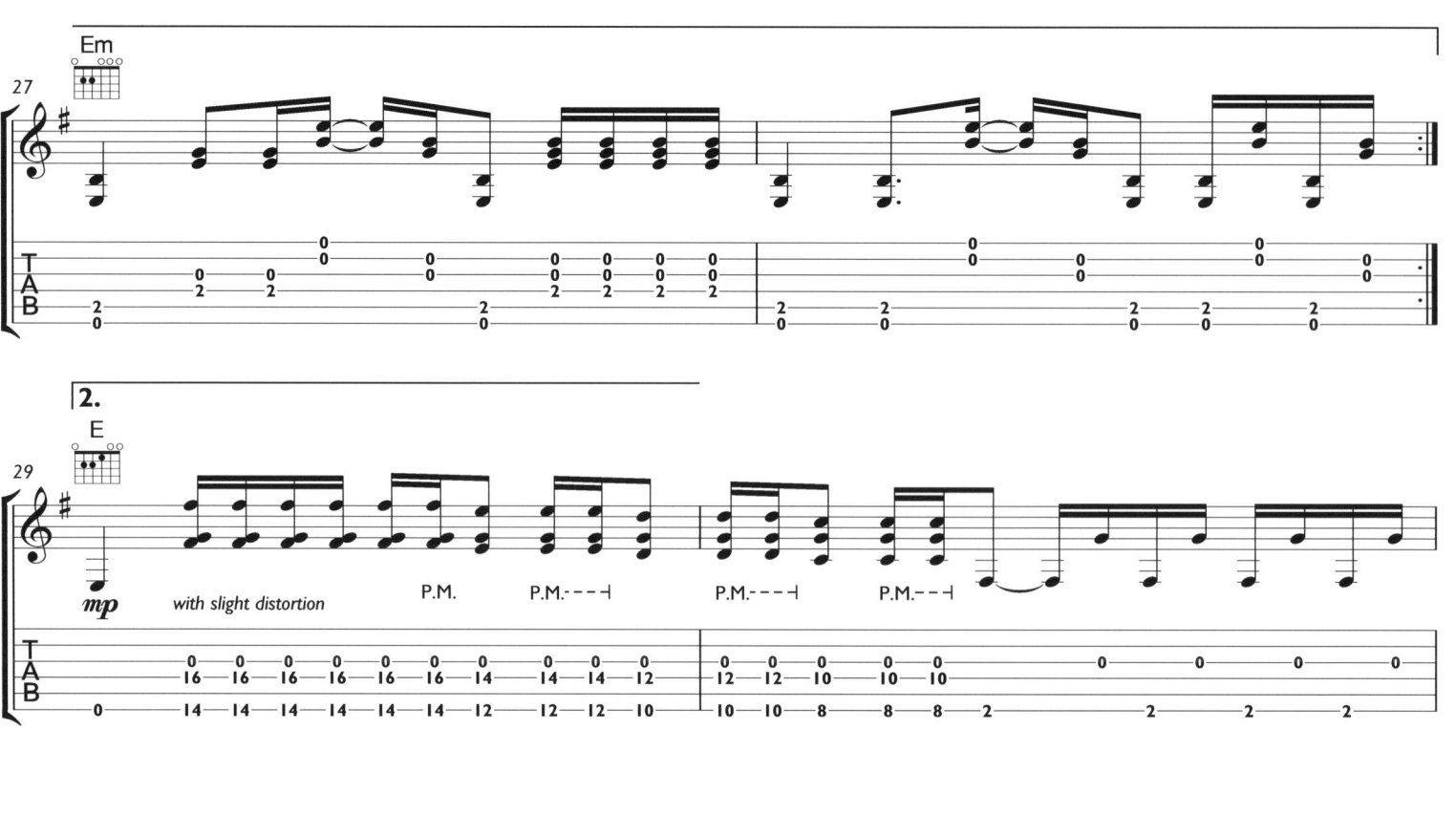
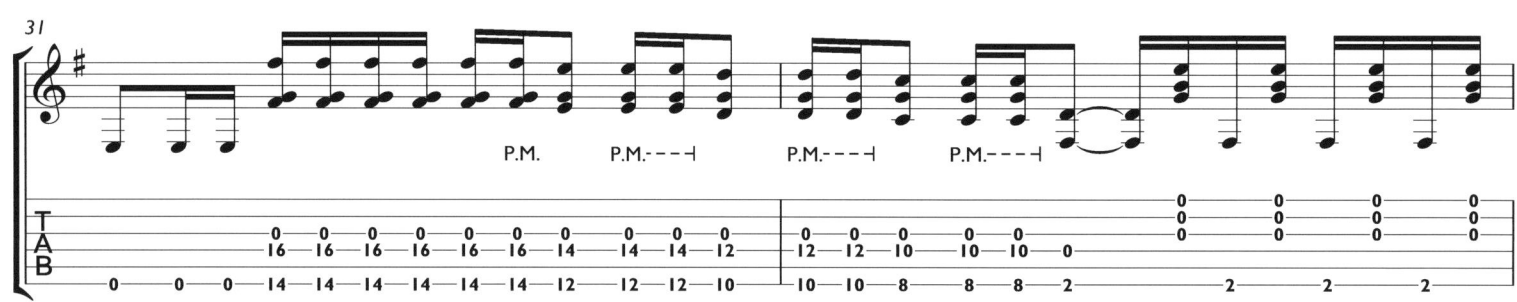
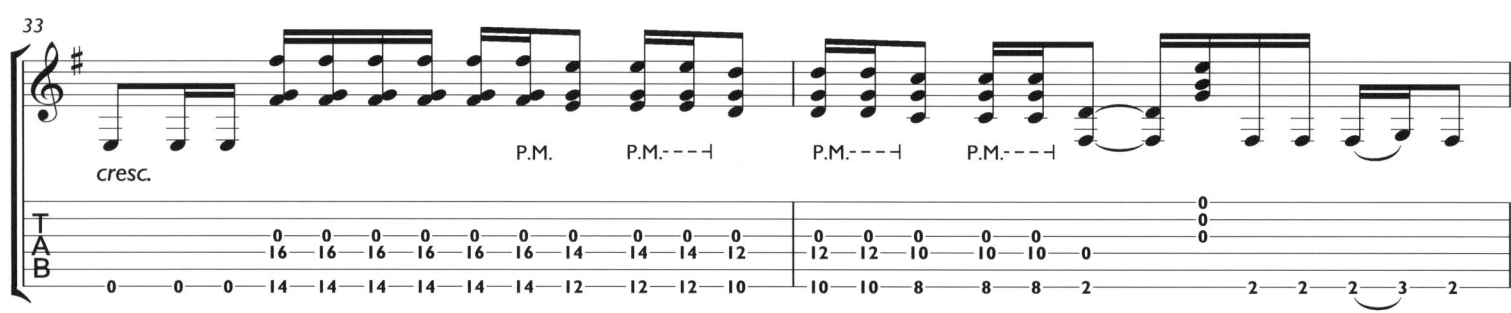
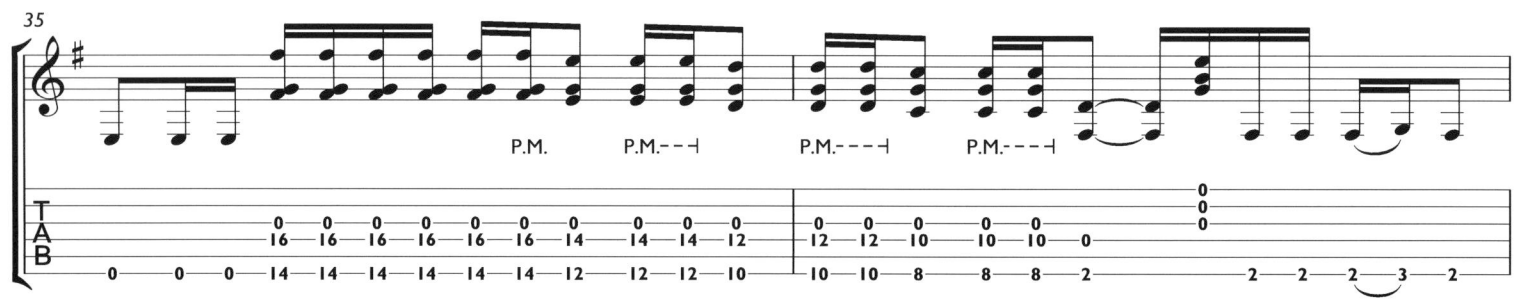

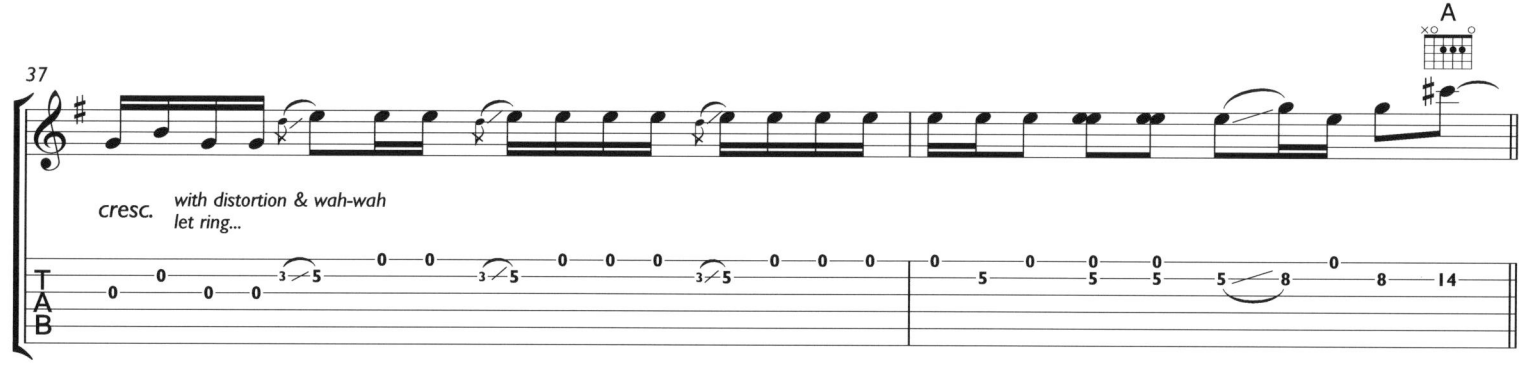

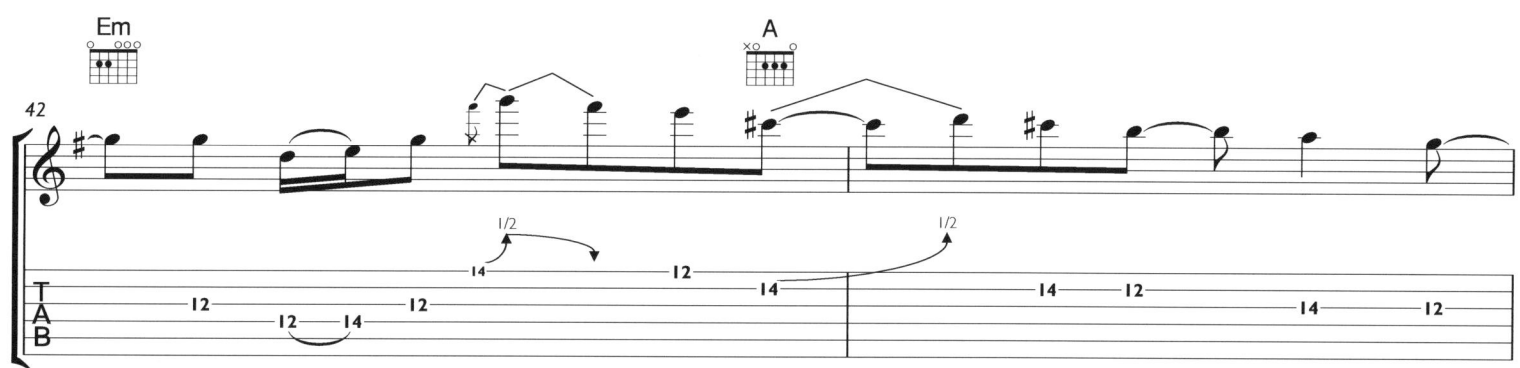
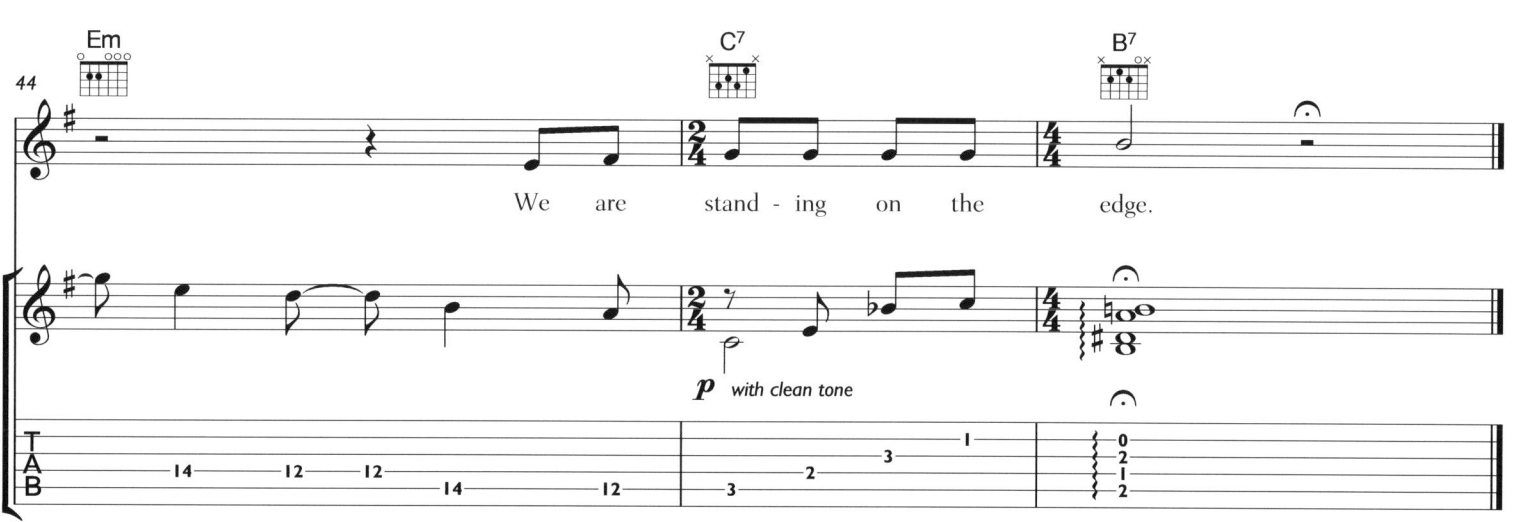

We are stand-ing on the edge.

THE TOURIST

**Words and Music by Thomas Yorke, Colin Greenwood,
Jonathan Greenwood, Edward O'Brien and Philip Selway**

Tune guitar:
1 = E   4 = E
2 = B   5 = A
3 = G   6 = E (lowest string)

♩. = 76

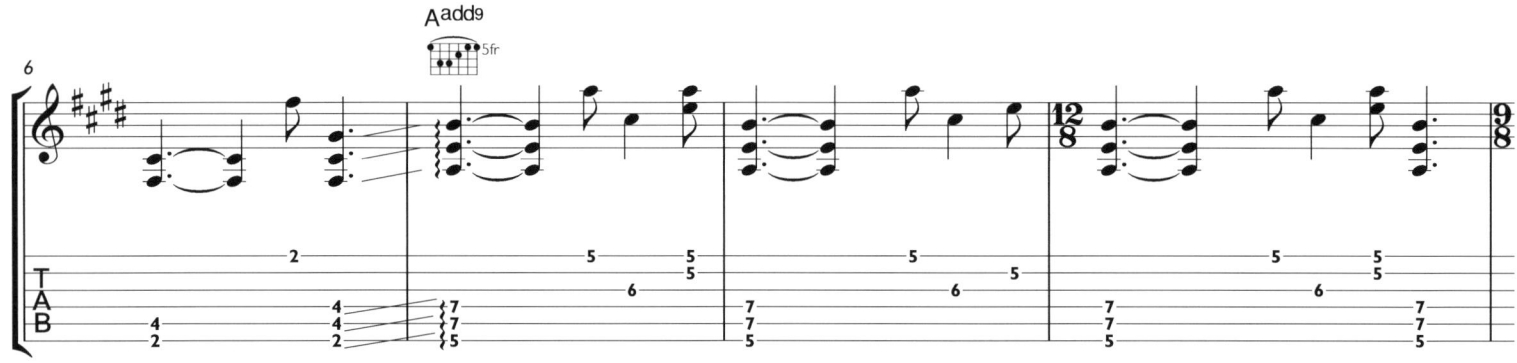

© 1997 Warner/Chappell Music Ltd
All Rights Reserved.

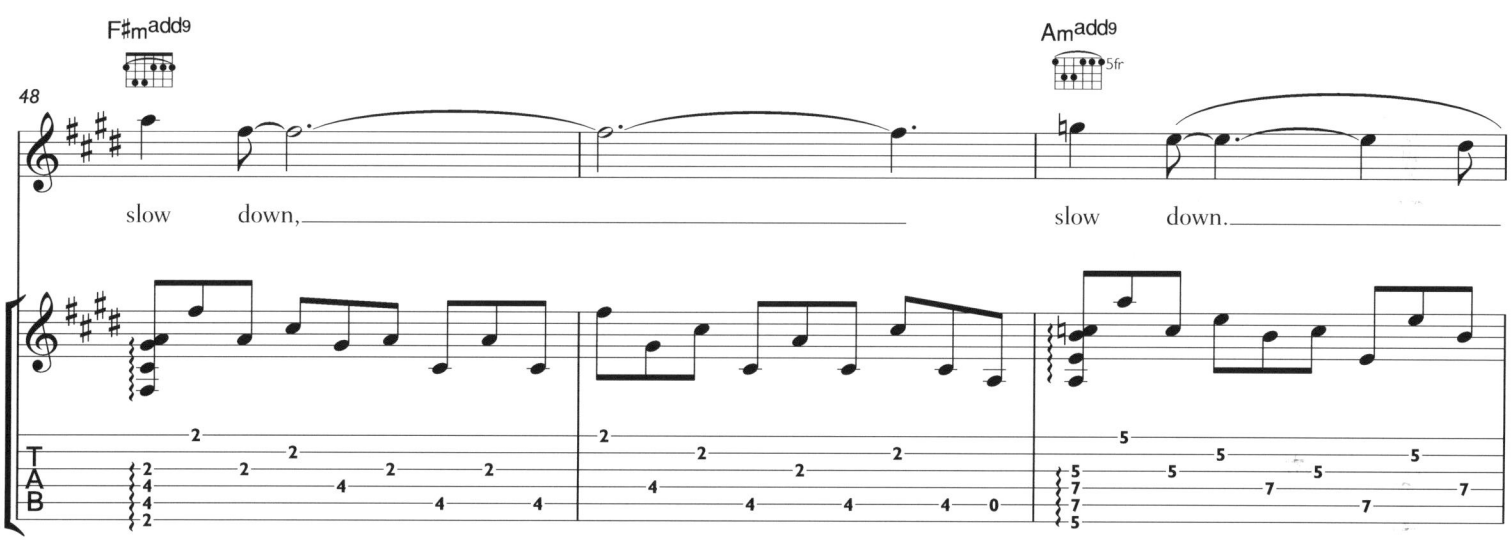

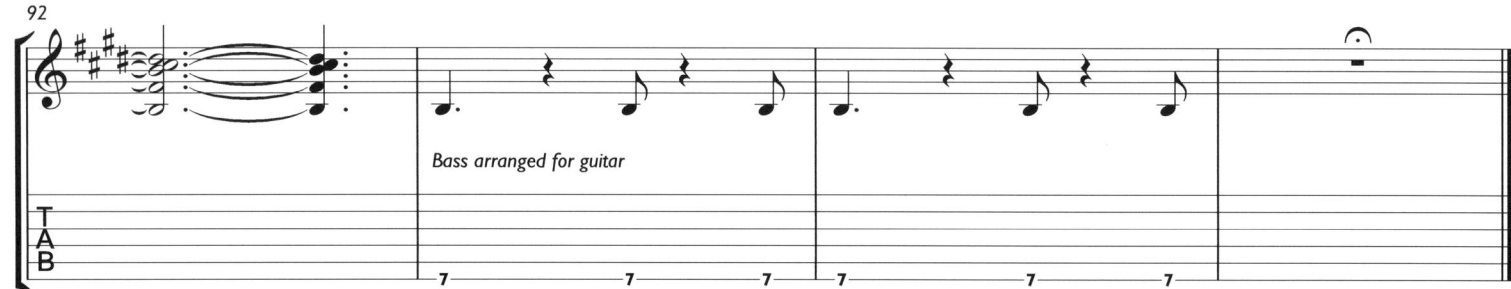

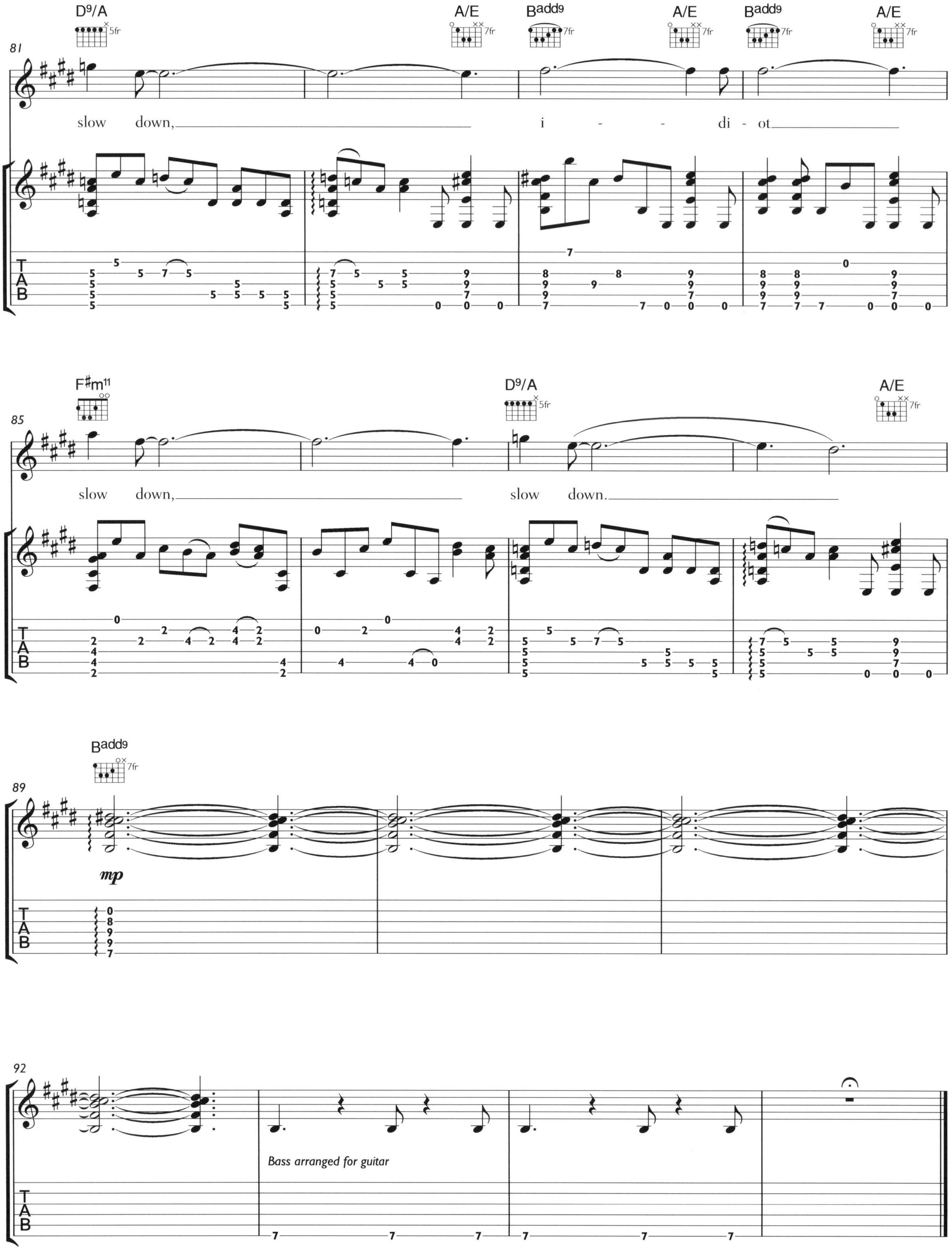
D9/A
A/E
Badd9
A/E
Badd9
A/E
81
slow down,
i - - di - ot
F♯m11
D9/A
A/E
85
slow down,
slow down.
Badd9
89
mp
92
Bass arranged for guitar

I PROMISE

Words and Music by Thomas Yorke, Jonathan Greenwood, Colin Greenwood, Edward O'Brien and Philip Selway

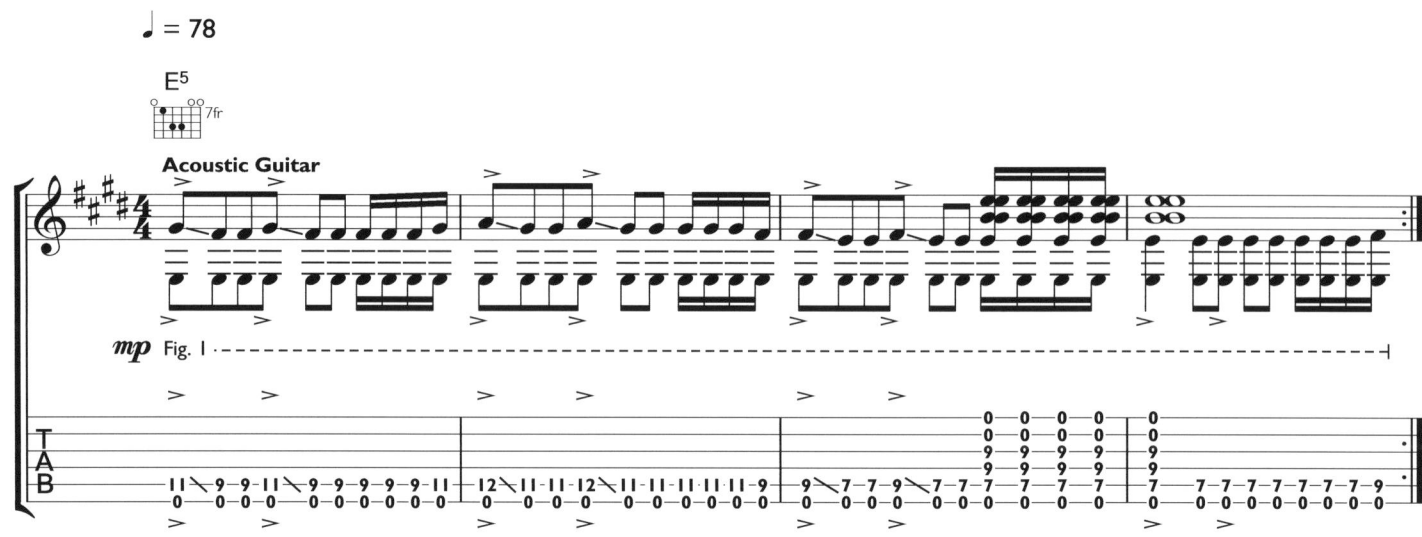

© 1997 Warner/Chappell Music Ltd
All Rights Reserved.

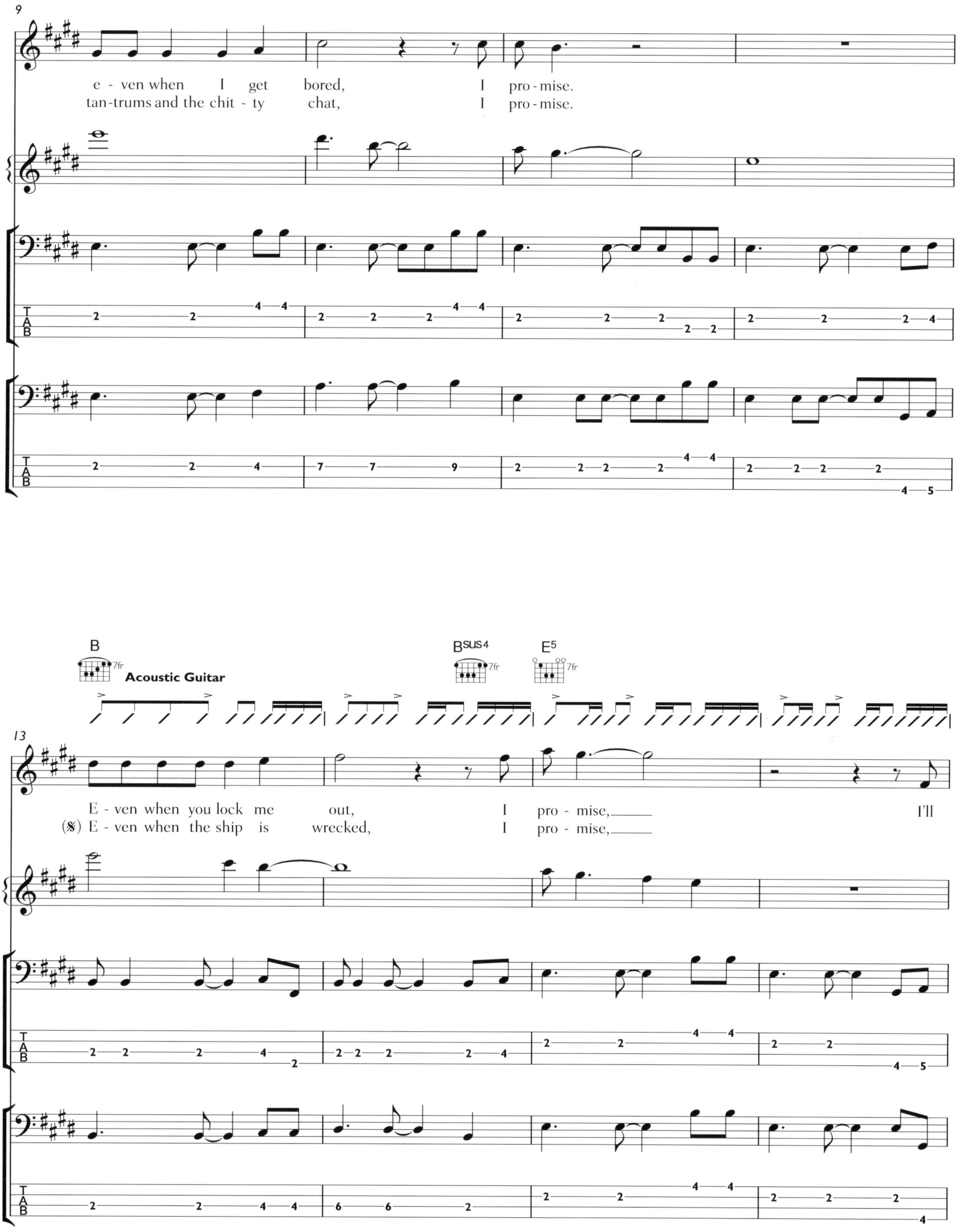
9
e - ven when I get bored, I pro - mise.
tan-trums and the chit - ty chat, I pro - mise.
B
Bsus4
E5
7fr
Acoustic Guitar
13
E - ven when you lock me out, I pro - mise, I'll
(𝄋) E - ven when the ship is wrecked, I pro - mise,

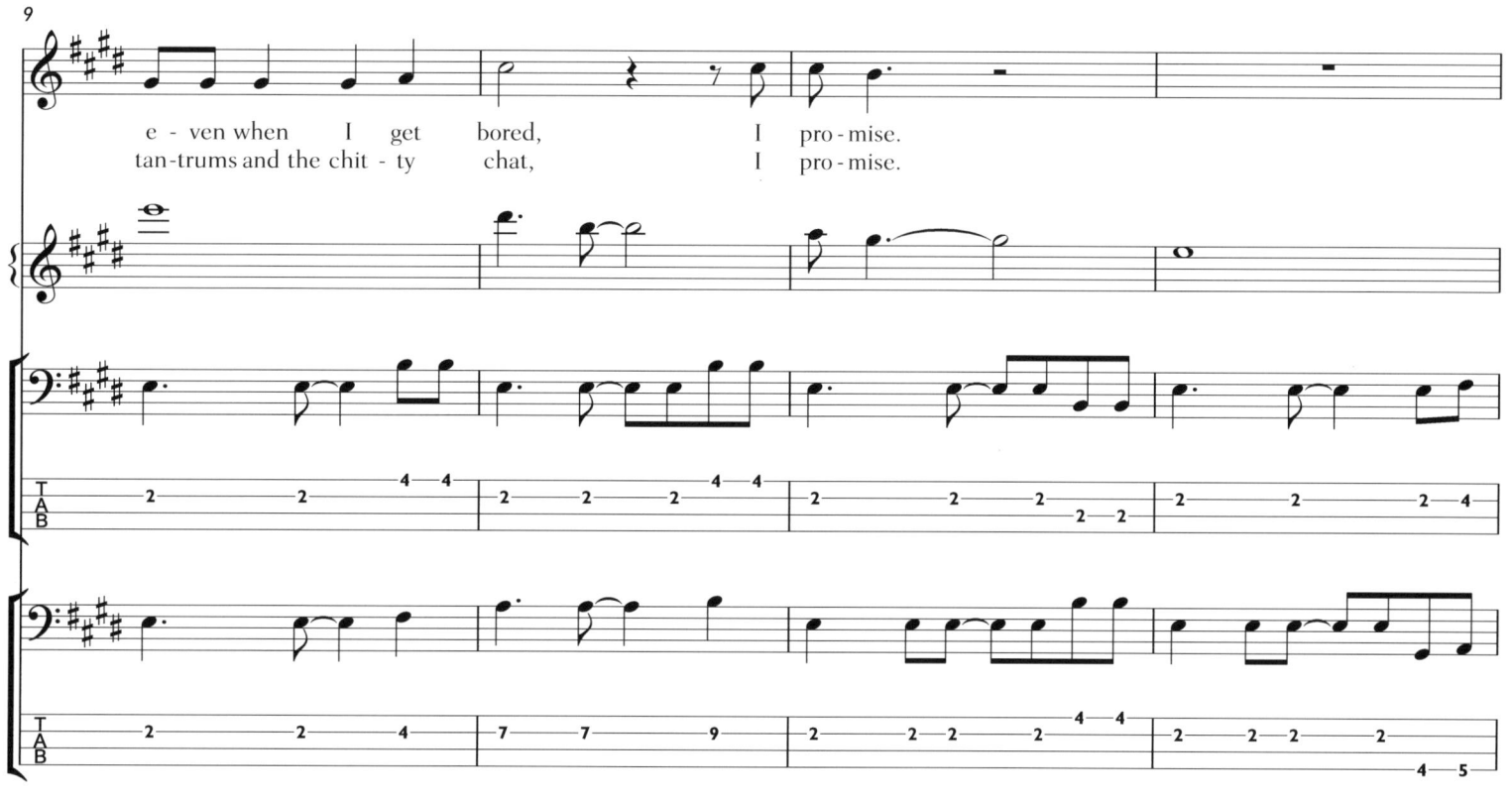

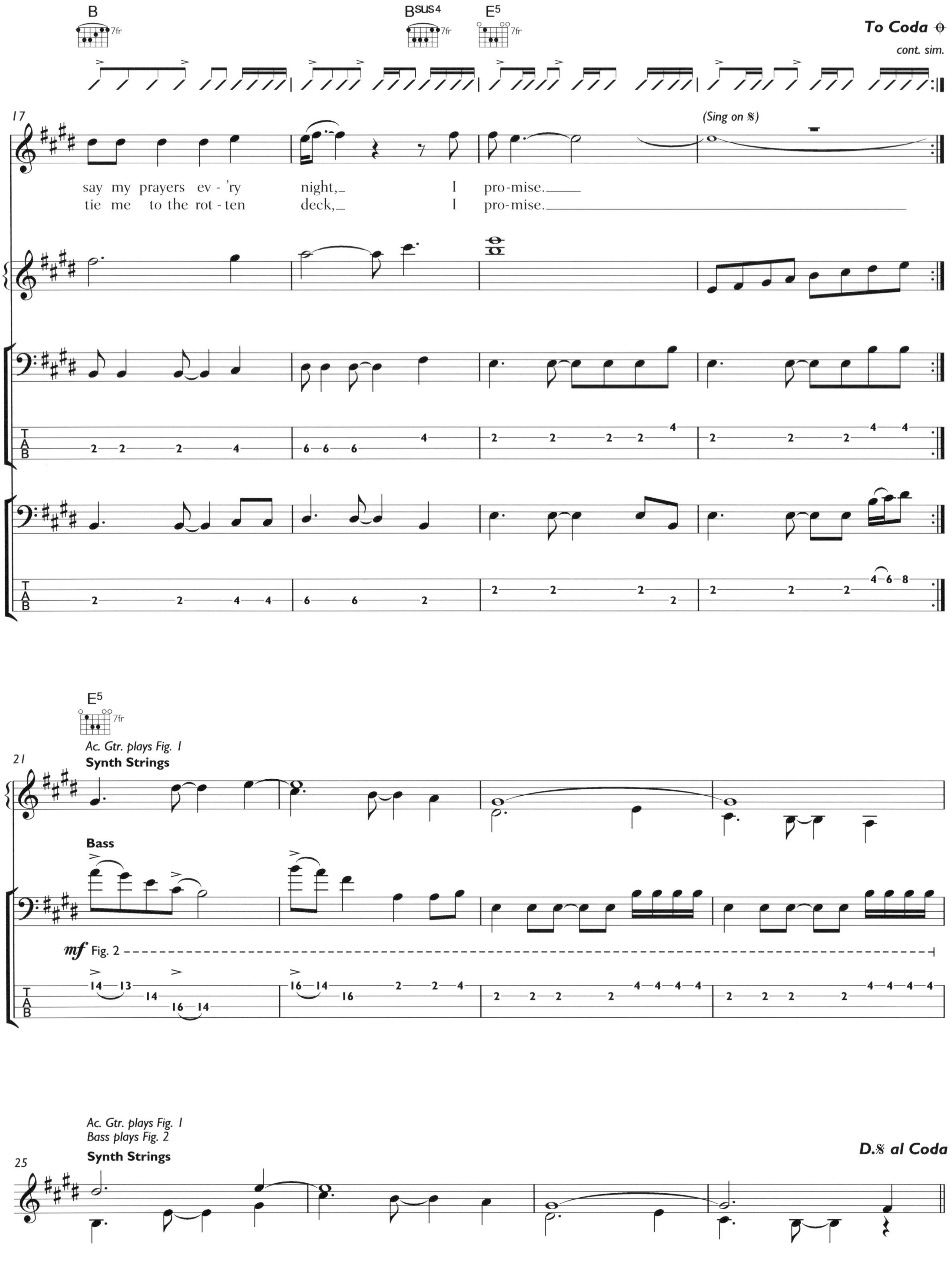
B
Bsus4
E5
7fr
To Coda
cont. sim.
17
(Sing on 𝄋)
say my prayers ev - 'ry night, I pro-mise.
tie me to the rot - ten deck, I pro-mise.
E5
Ac. Gtr. plays Fig. 1
Synth Strings
21
Bass
mf Fig. 2
Ac. Gtr. plays Fig. 1
Bass plays Fig. 2
Synth Strings
25
D.𝄋 al Coda

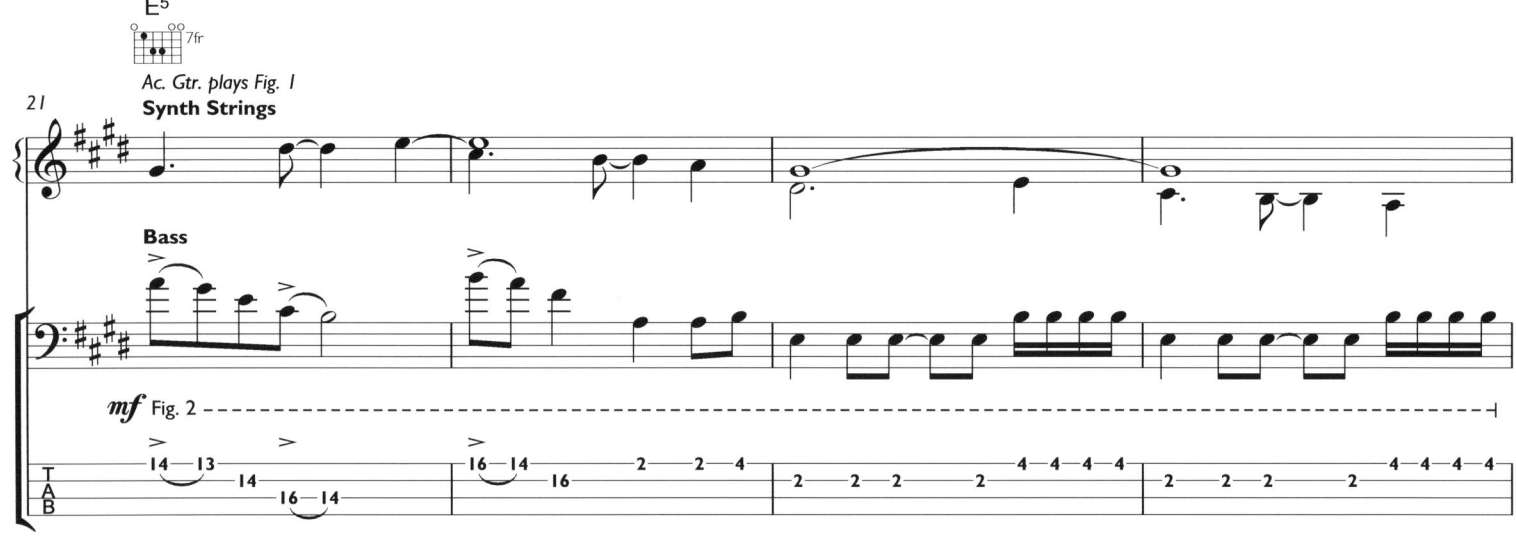

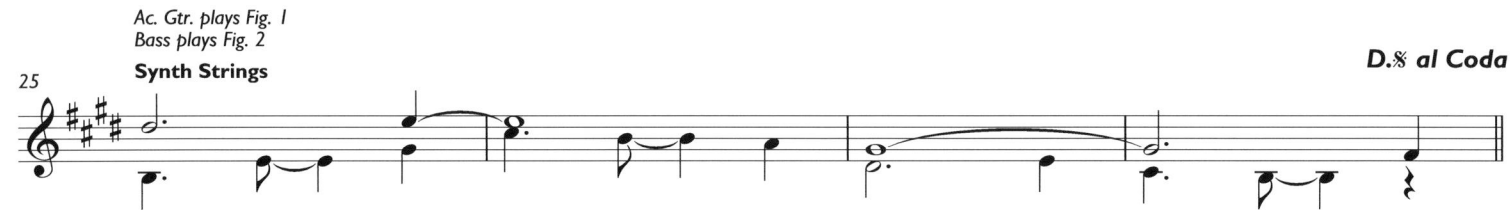

MAN OF WAR

**Words and Music by Thomas Yorke, Jonathan Greenwood,
Colin Greenwood, Edward O'Brien and Philip Selway**

© 1997 Warner/Chappell Music Ltd
All Rights Reserved.

Am
D7/F♯
F
25
D7/F♯
C
C/B
Am7
C/G
28
Yeah, the worms will come for you,
p
Bass
Piano

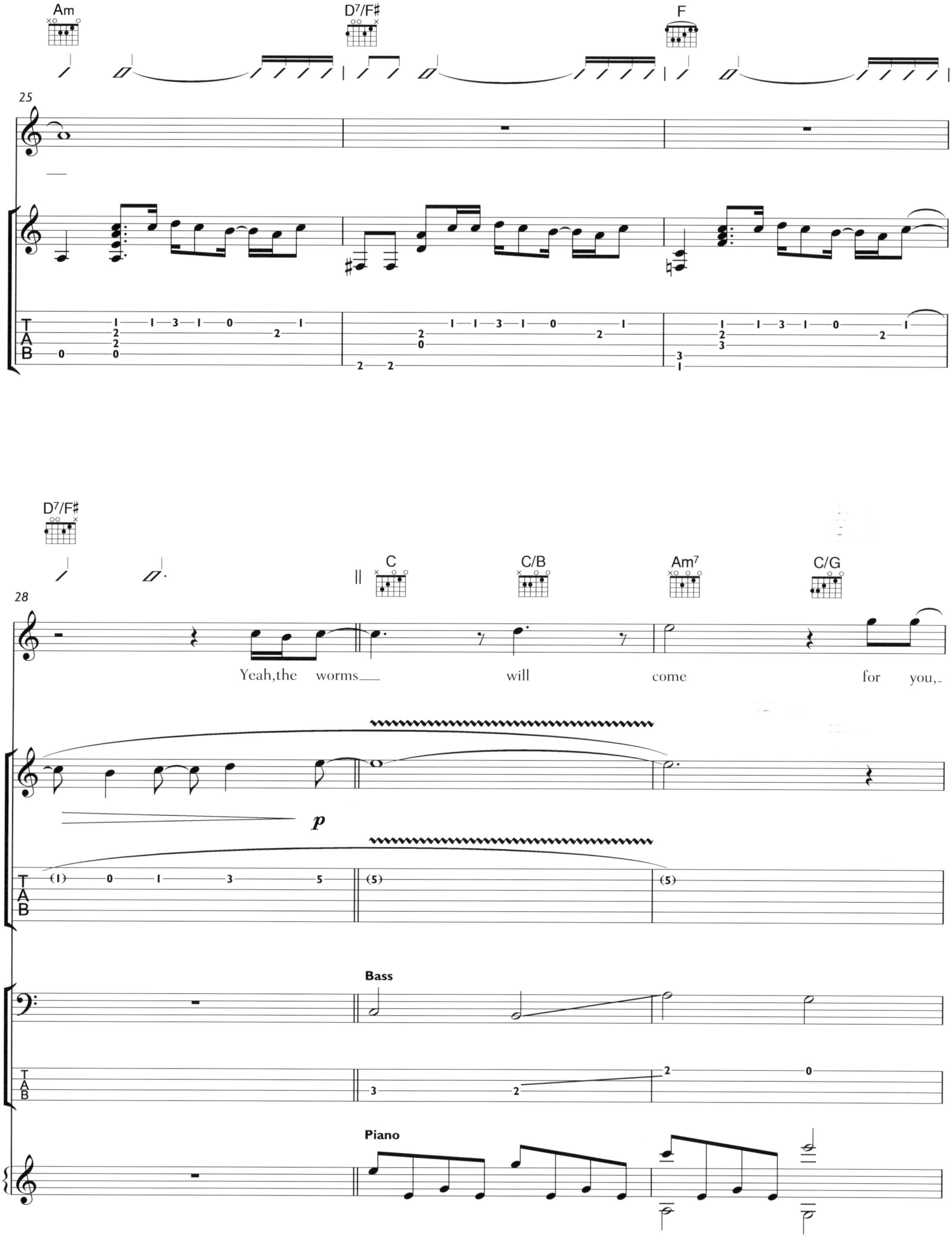

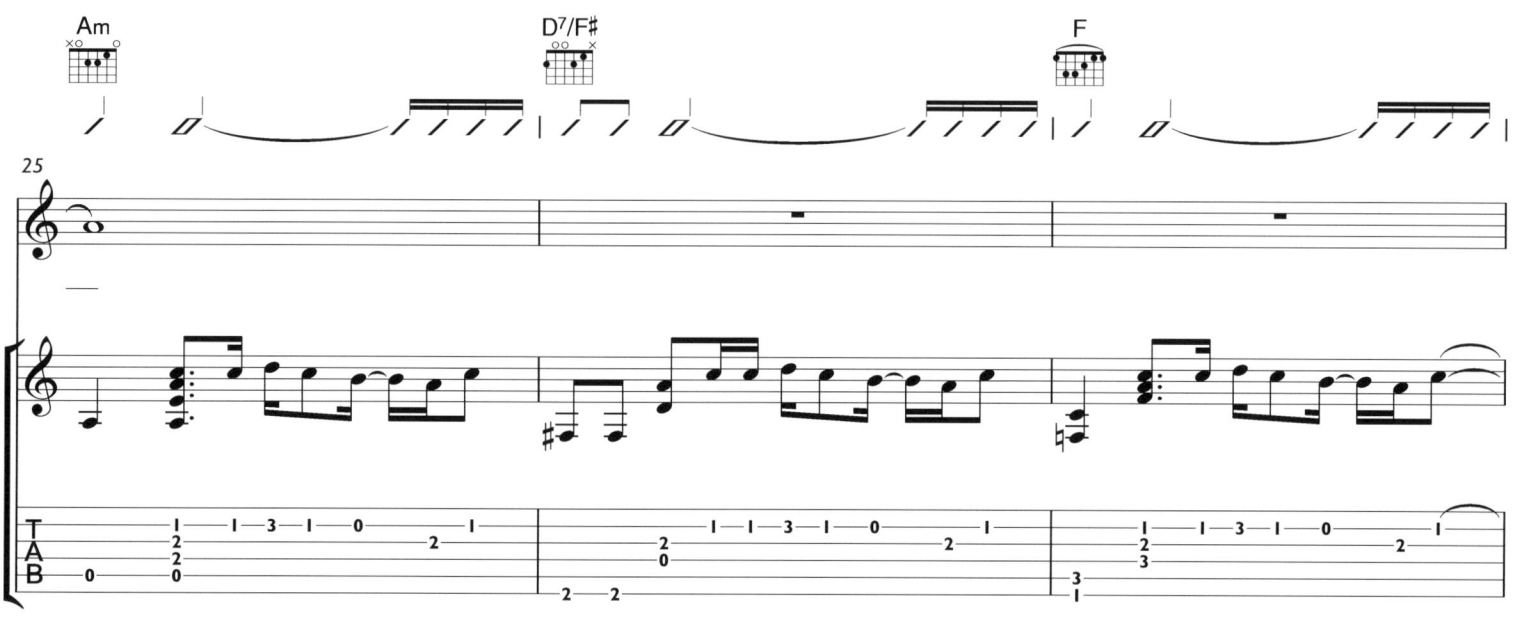

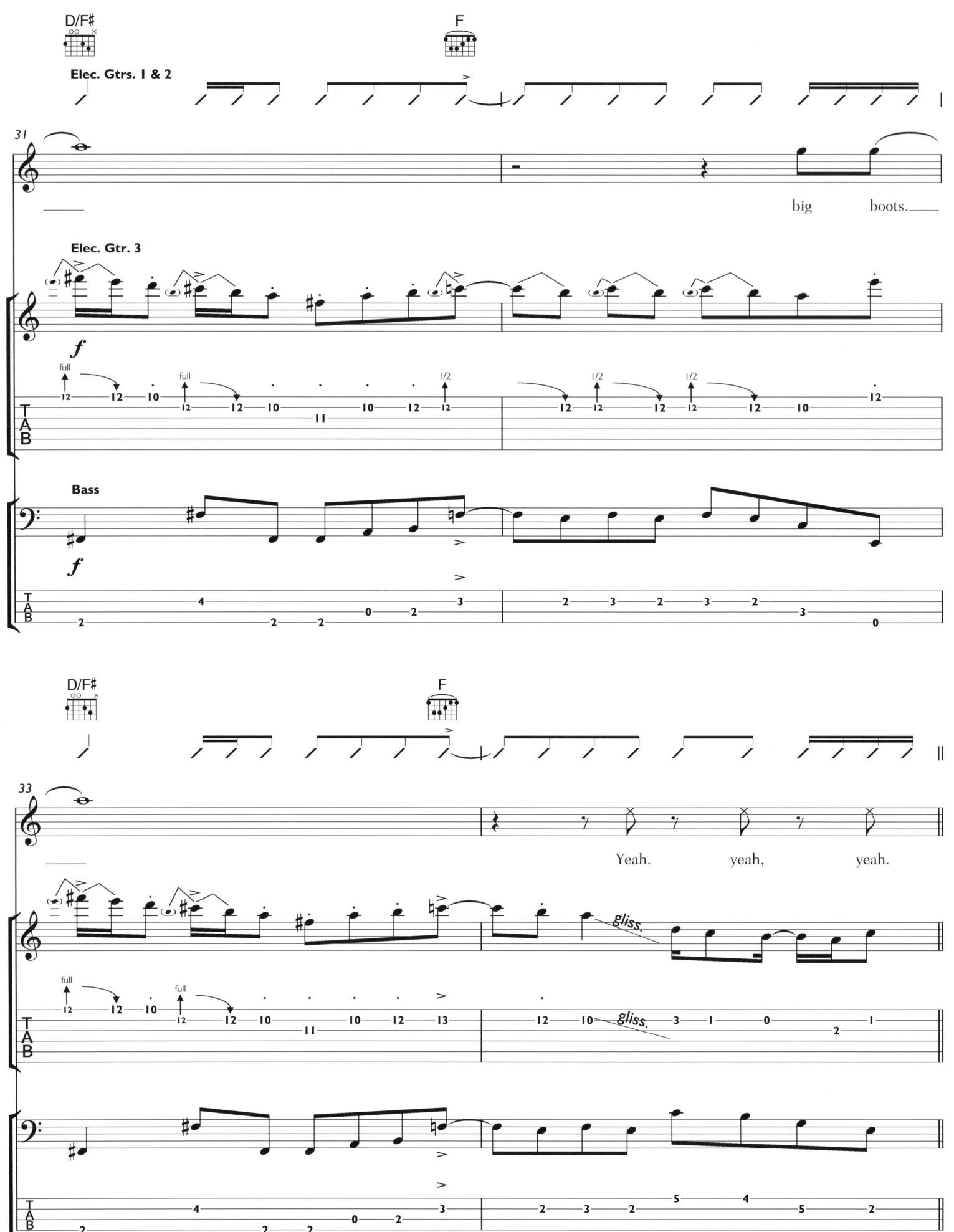

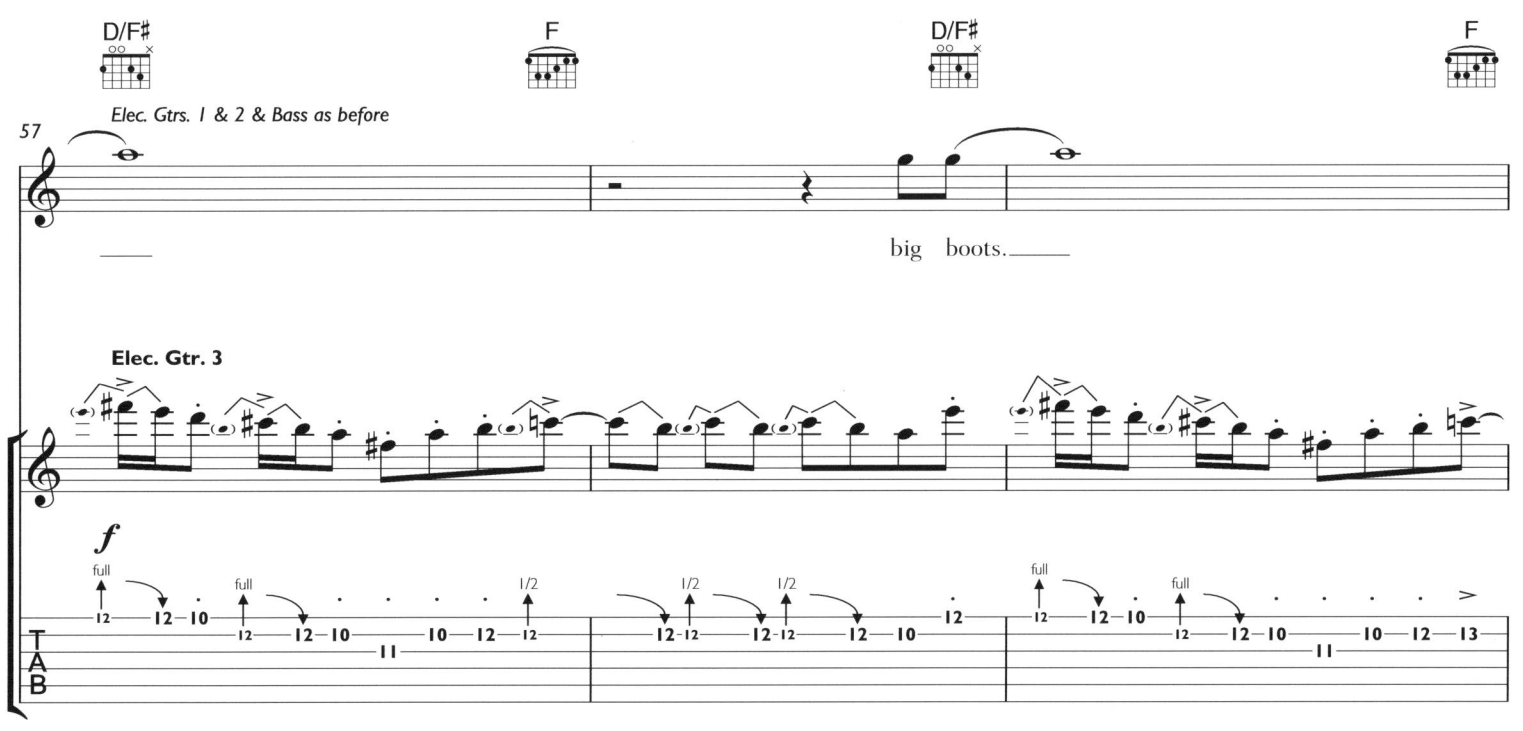

Am
G
Fmaj7
Elec. Gtr. 1
with clean tone
63
big boots,
for you,
Elec. Gtr. 3
with crunch & distant rev.
Piano
8va
67
big boots.
(8)

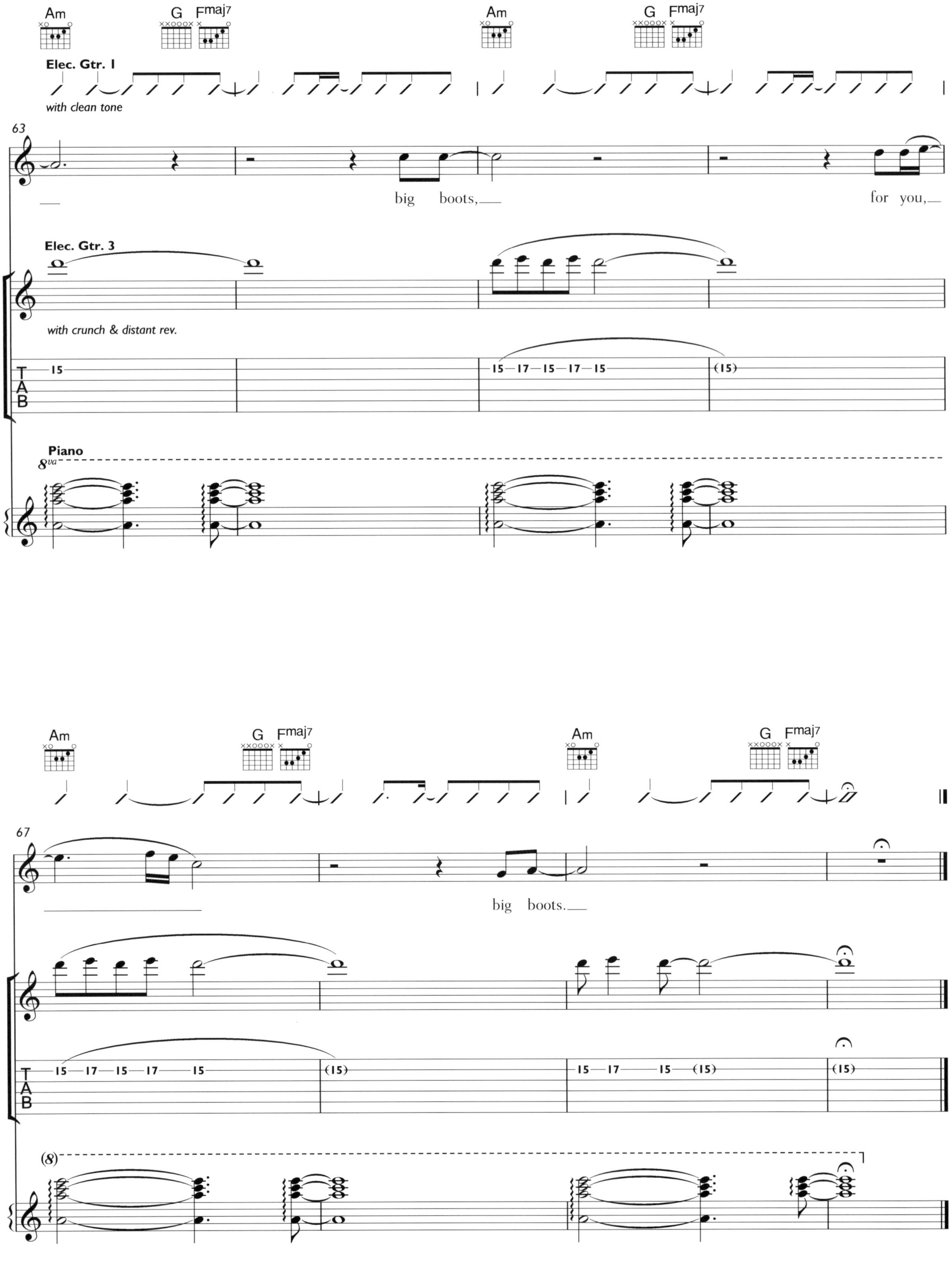

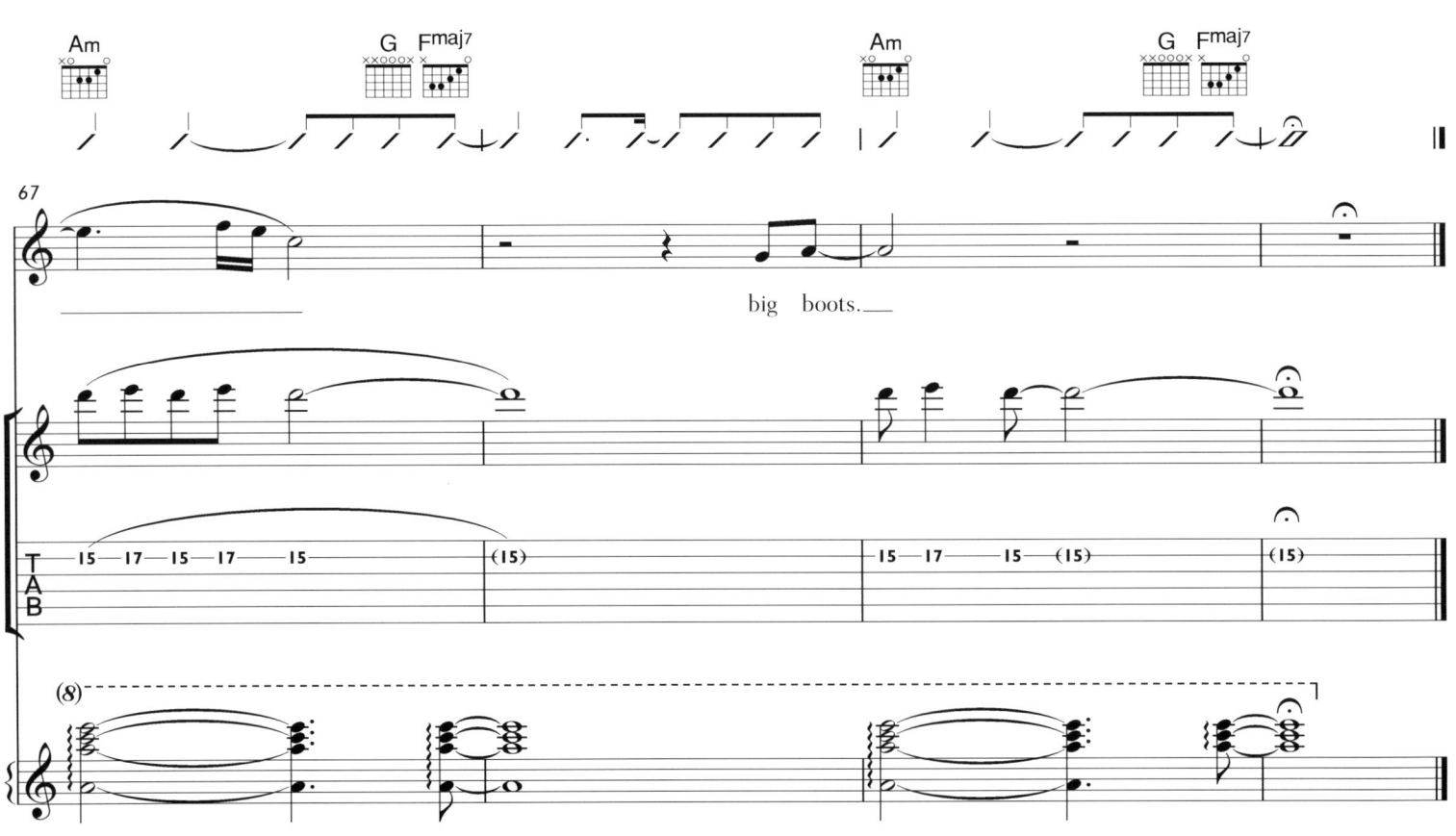

LIFT

Words and Music by Thomas Yorke, Jonathan Greenwood, Colin Greenwood, Edward O'Brien and Philip Selway

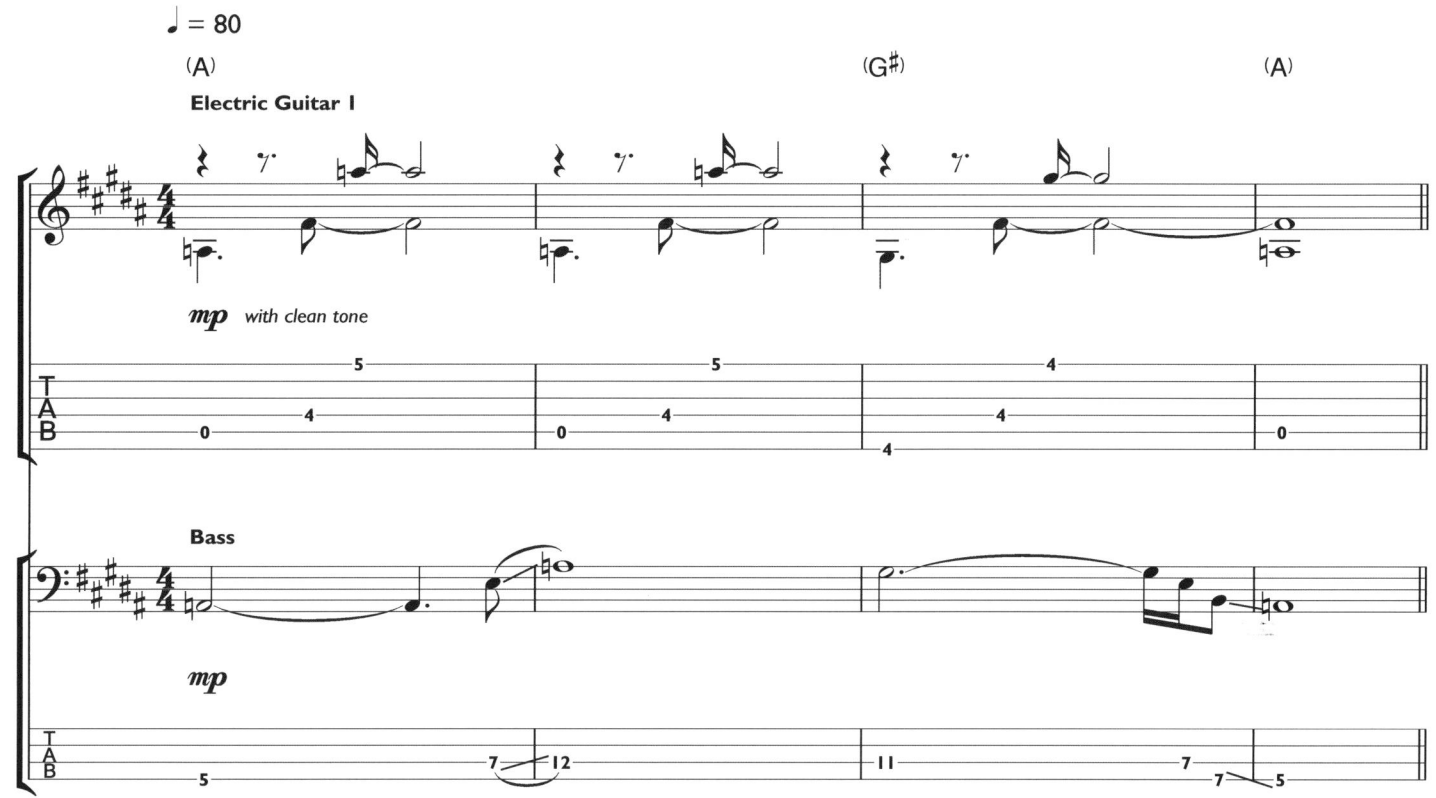

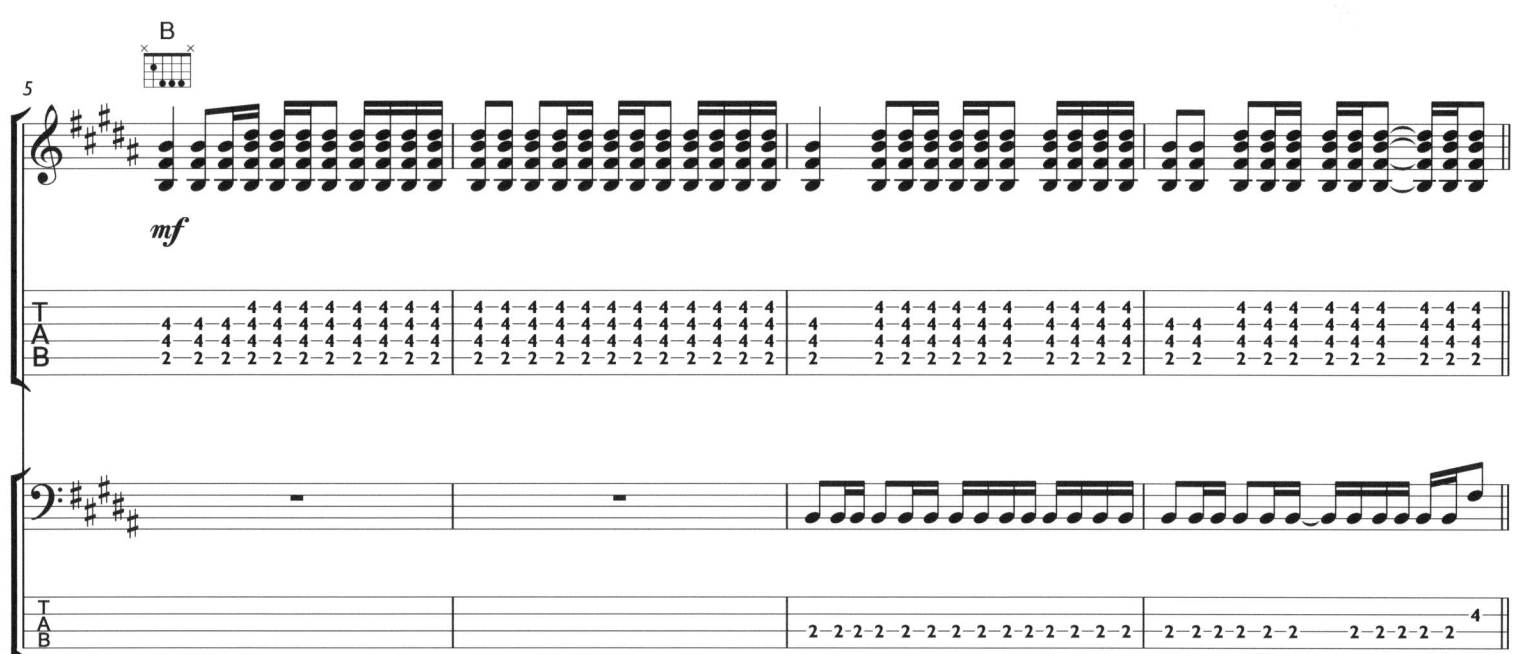

© 1997 Warner/Chappell Music Ltd
All Rights Reserved.

LULL

Words and Music by Thomas Yorke, Jonathan Greenwood, Colin Greenwood, Edward O'Brien and Philip Selway

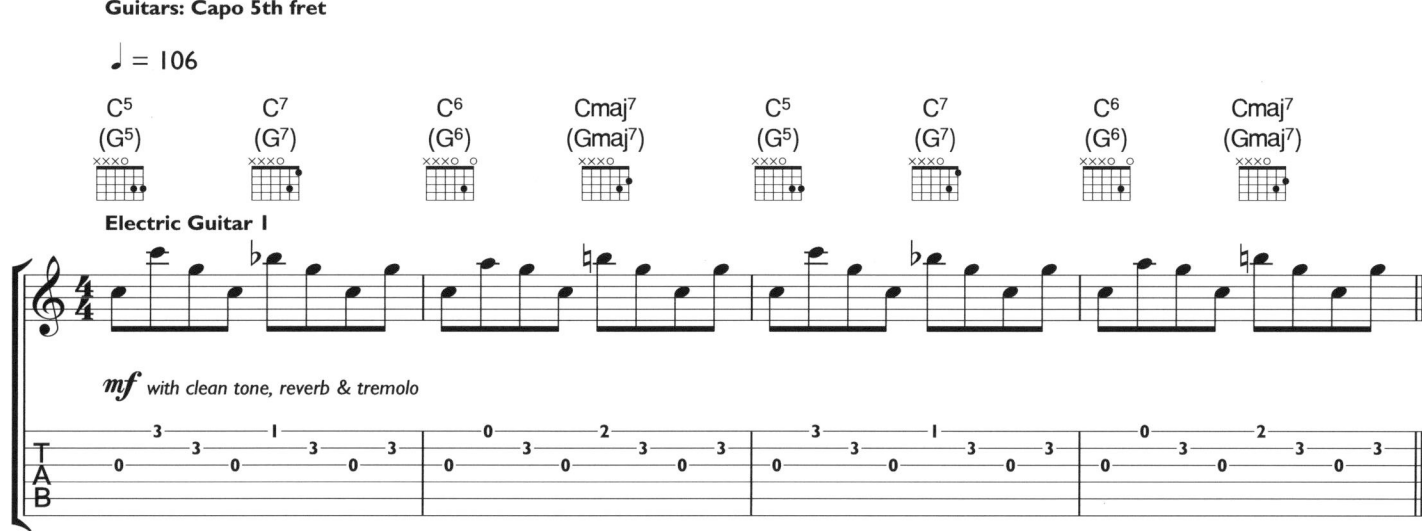

© 1997 Warner/Chappell Music Ltd
All Rights Reserved.

MEETING IN THE AISLE

Music by Thomas Yorke, Jonathan Greenwood, Colin Greenwood, Edward O'Brien and Philip Selway

MELATONIN

Words and Music by Thomas Yorke

© 1997 Warner/Chappell Music Ltd
All Rights Reserved.

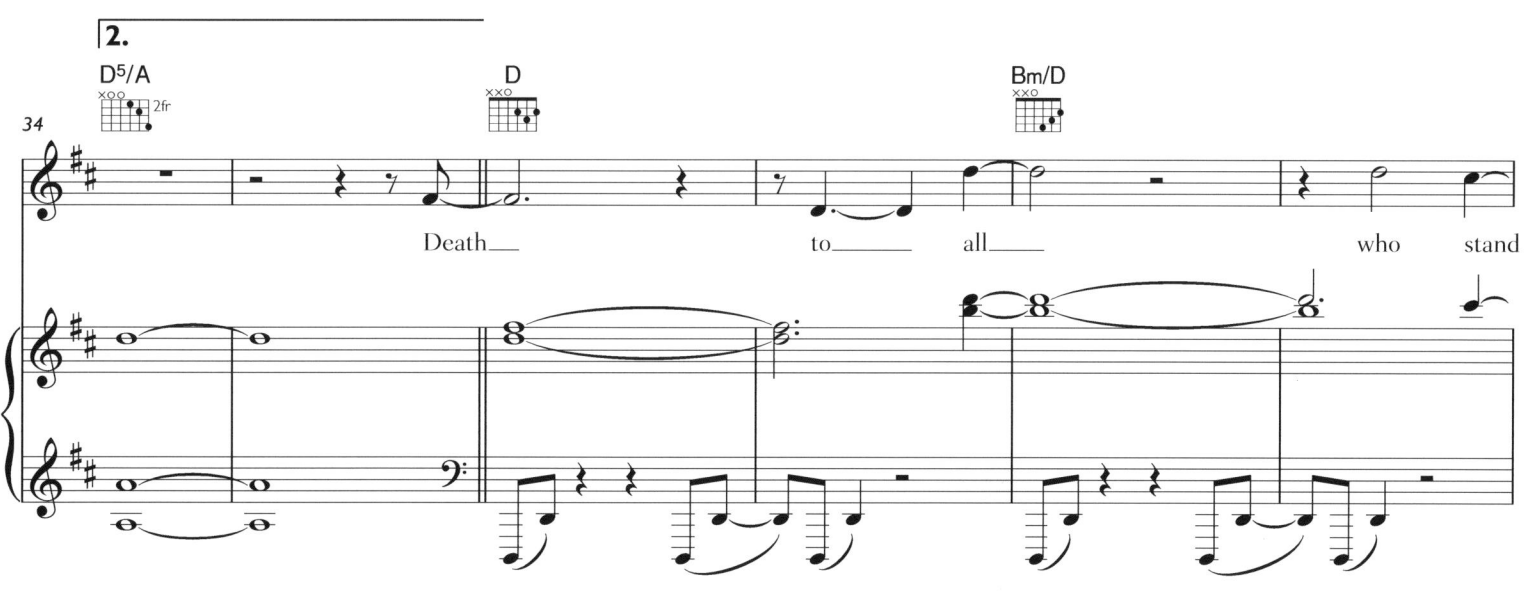

A REMINDER

Words and Music by Thomas Yorke, Jonathan Greenwood,
Colin Greenwood, Edward O'Brien and Philip Selway

© 1997 Warner/Chappell Music Ltd
All Rights Reserved.

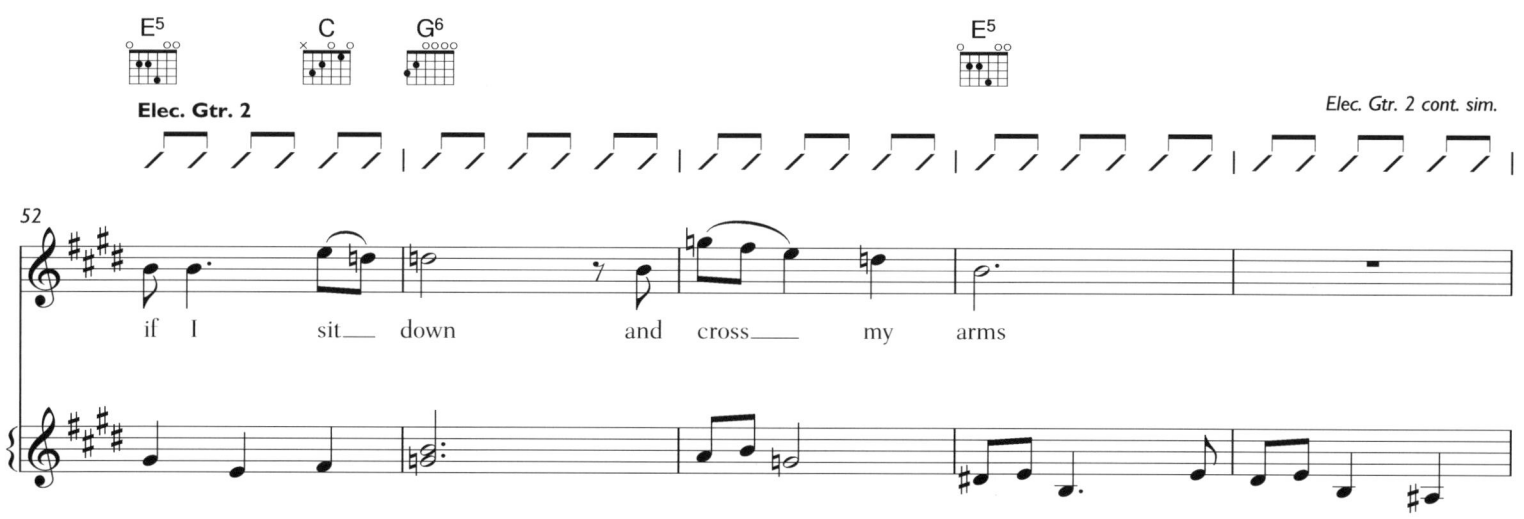

POLYETHYLENE (PARTS 1 & 2)

Words and Music by Thomas Yorke, Jonathan Greenwood,
Colin Greenwood, Edward O'Brien and Philip Selway

© 1997 Warner/Chappell Music Ltd
All Rights Reserved.

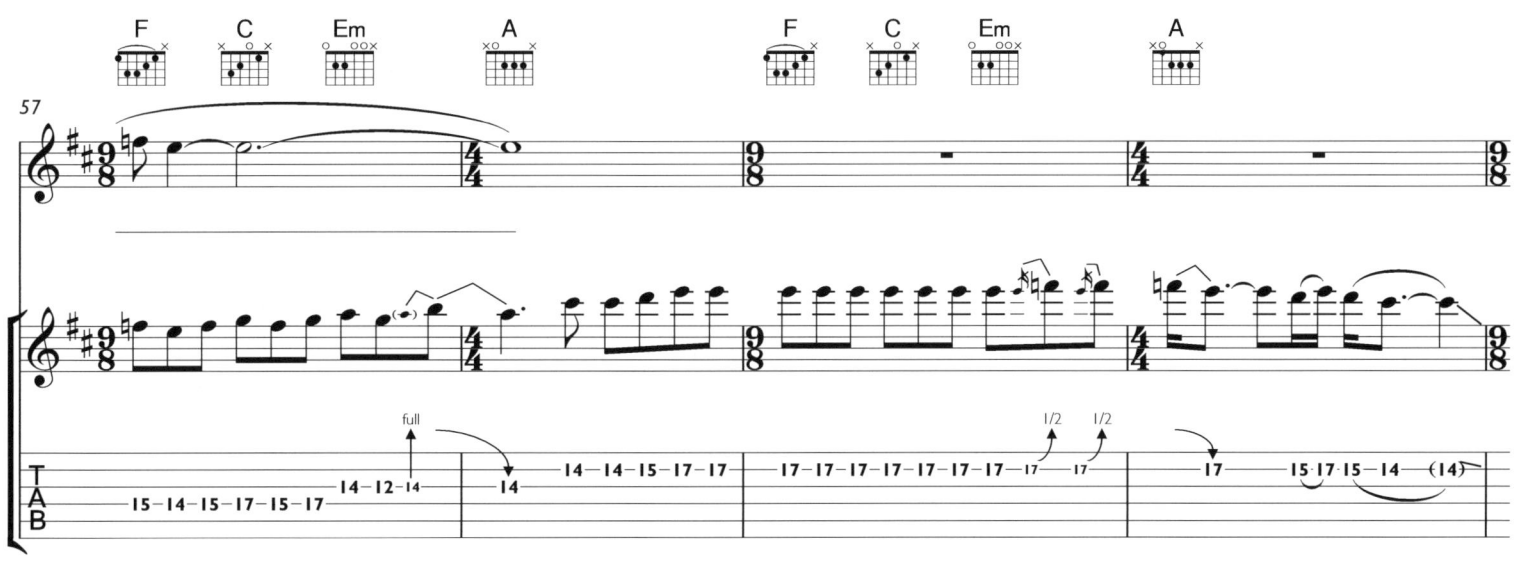
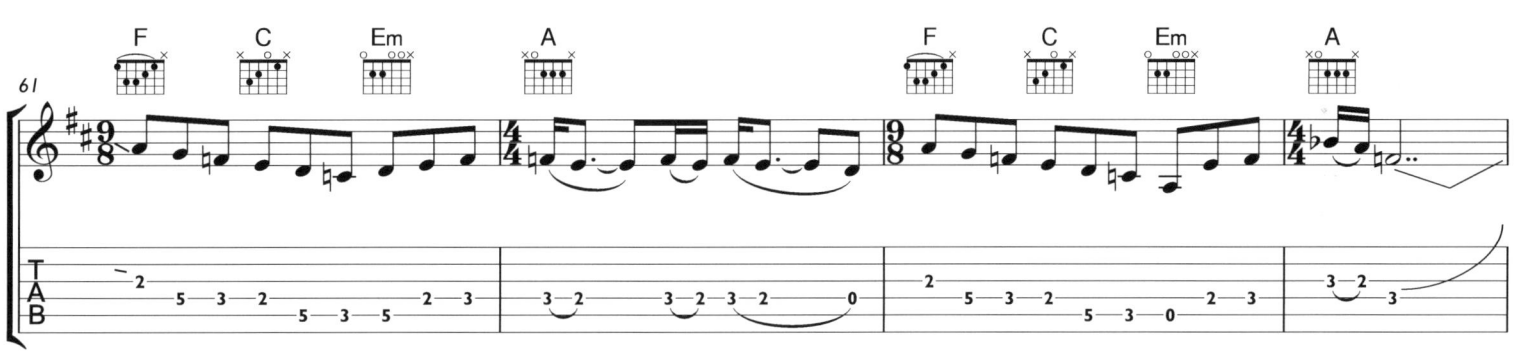
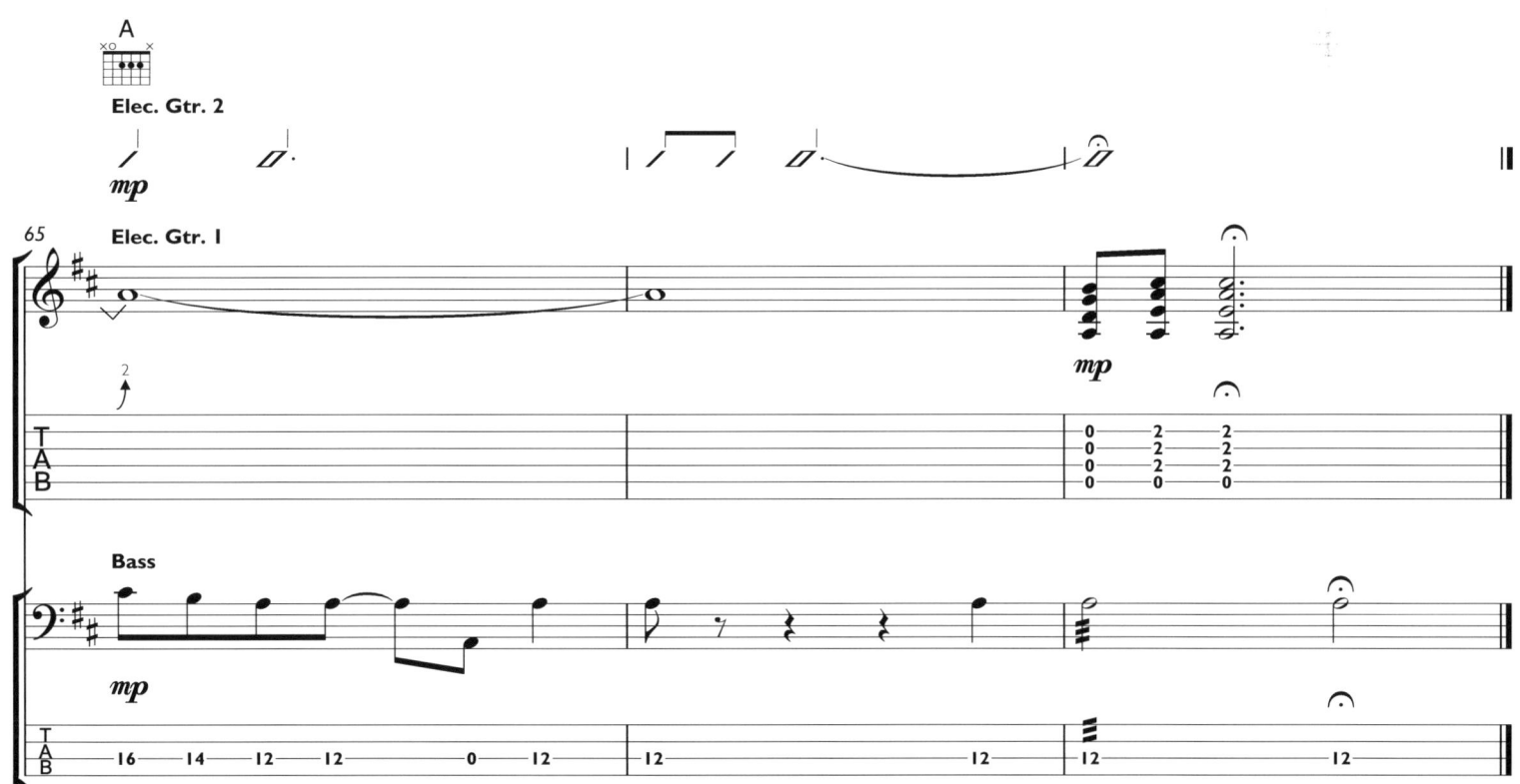

PEARLY

Words and Music by Thomas Yorke, Jonathan Greenwood, Colin Greenwood, Edward O'Brien and Philip Selway

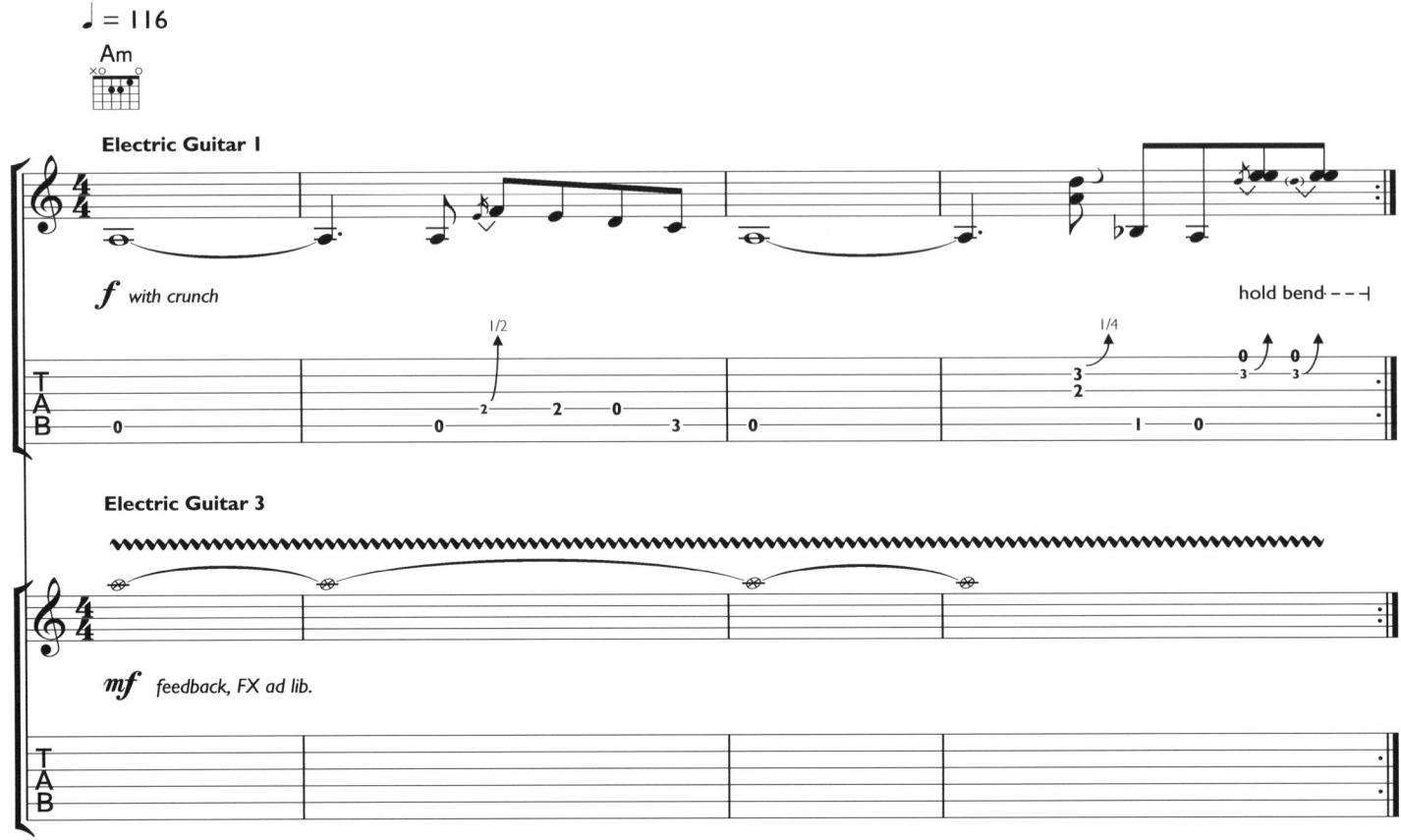

© 1997 Warner/Chappell Music Ltd
All Rights Reserved.

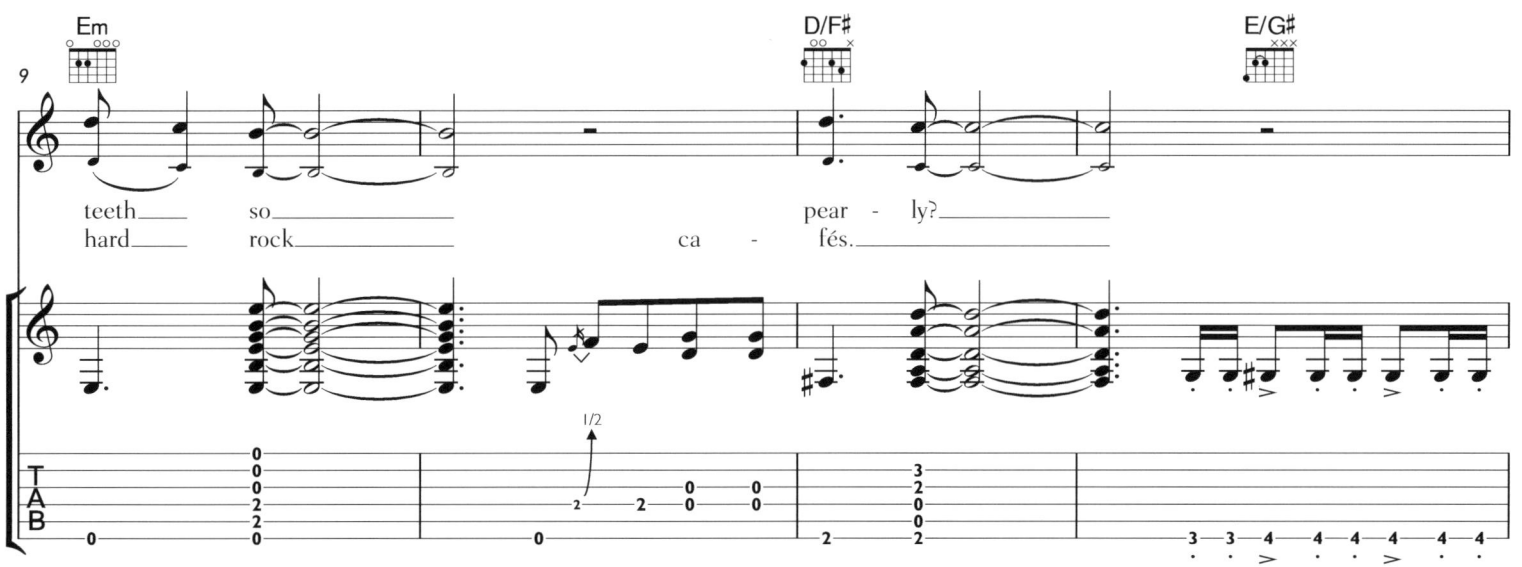

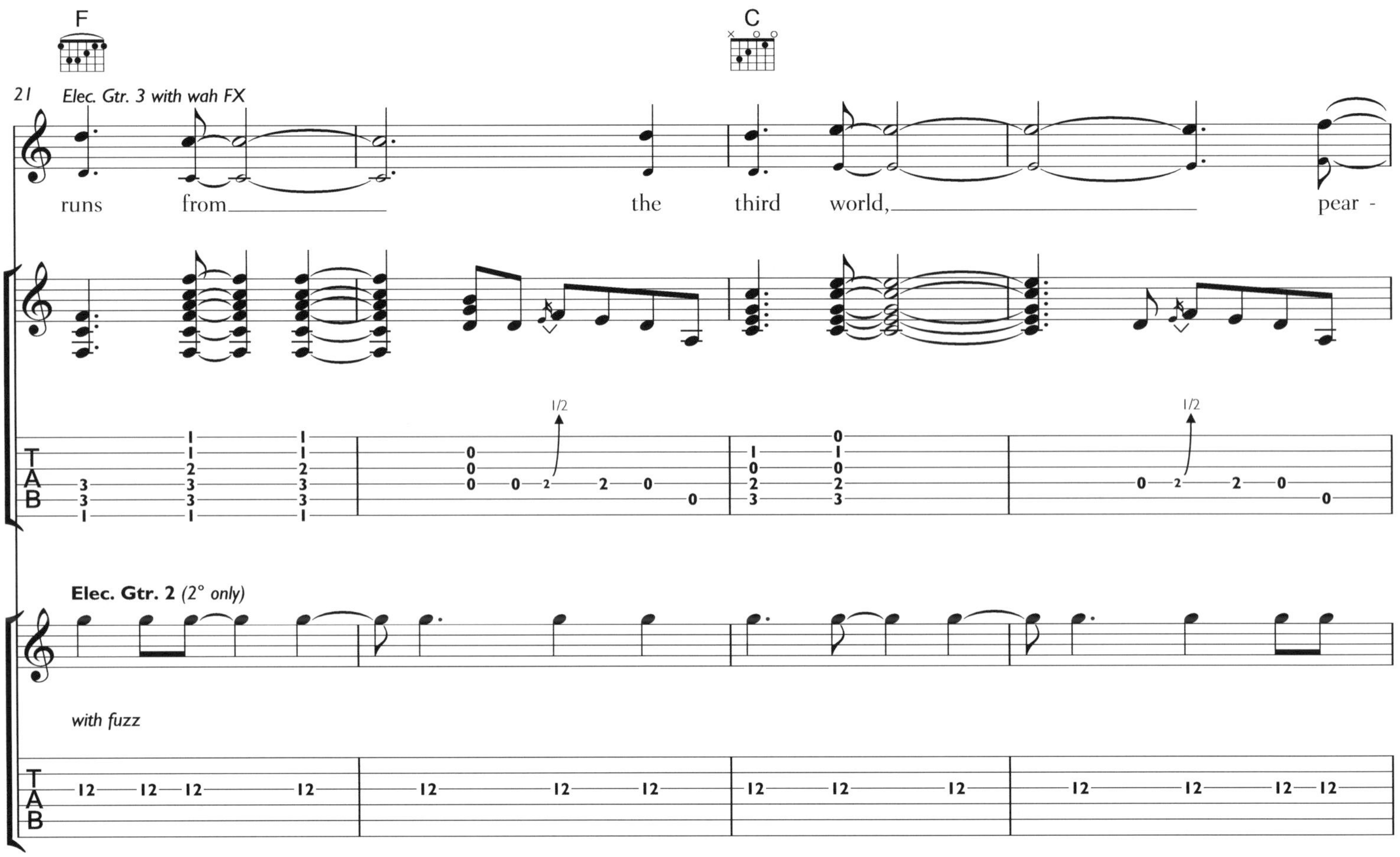
F
C
21
Elec. Gtr. 3 with wah FX
runs from the third world, pear -
1/2
1/2
Elec. Gtr. 2 (2° only)
with fuzz

E
Elec. Gtr. 1
2fr
2fr
25
(Sing 1° only)
- - - - - - - ly.
2. Va -
Elec. Gtr. 2 (both times)

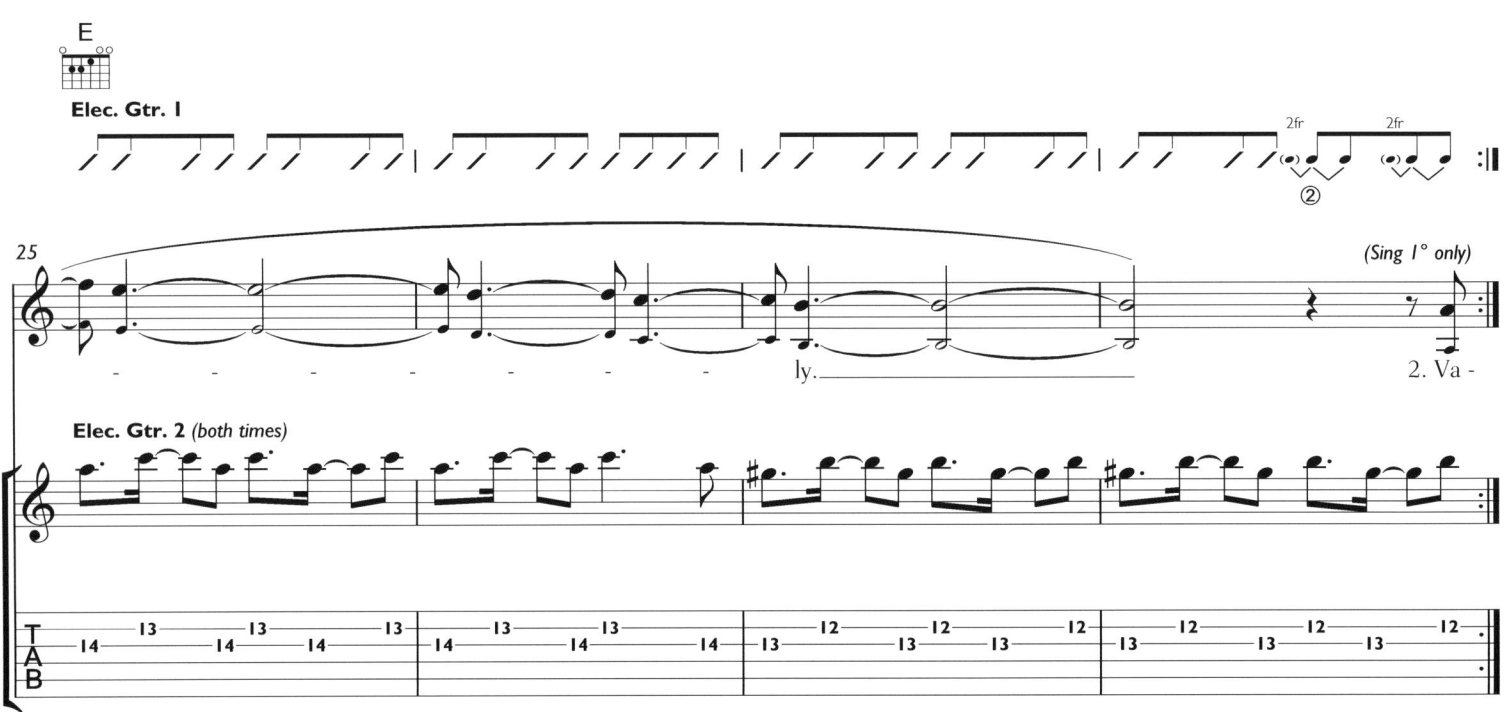

PALO ALTO

Words and Music by Thomas Yorke, Jonathan Greenwood,
Colin Greenwood, Edward O'Brien and Philip Selway

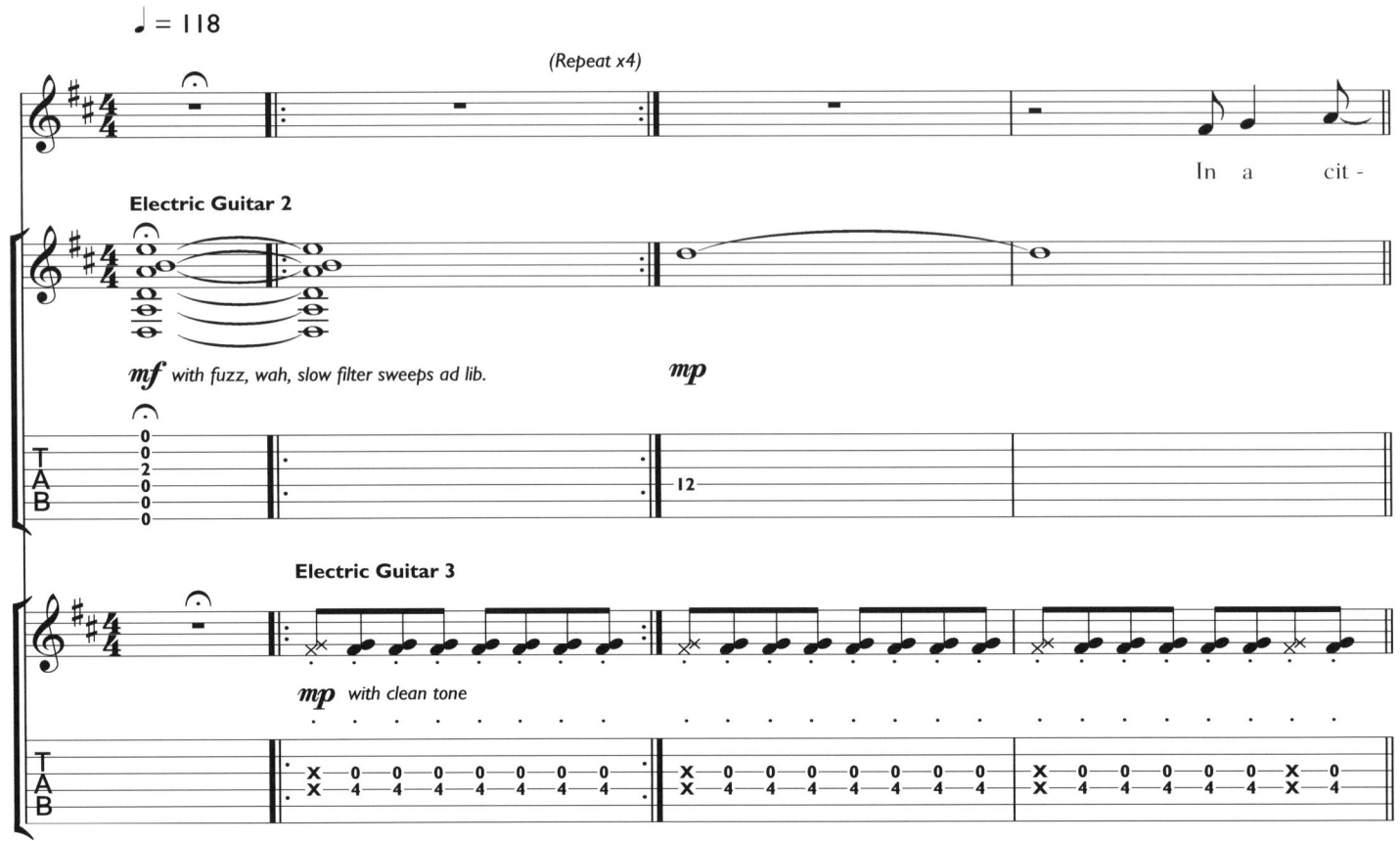

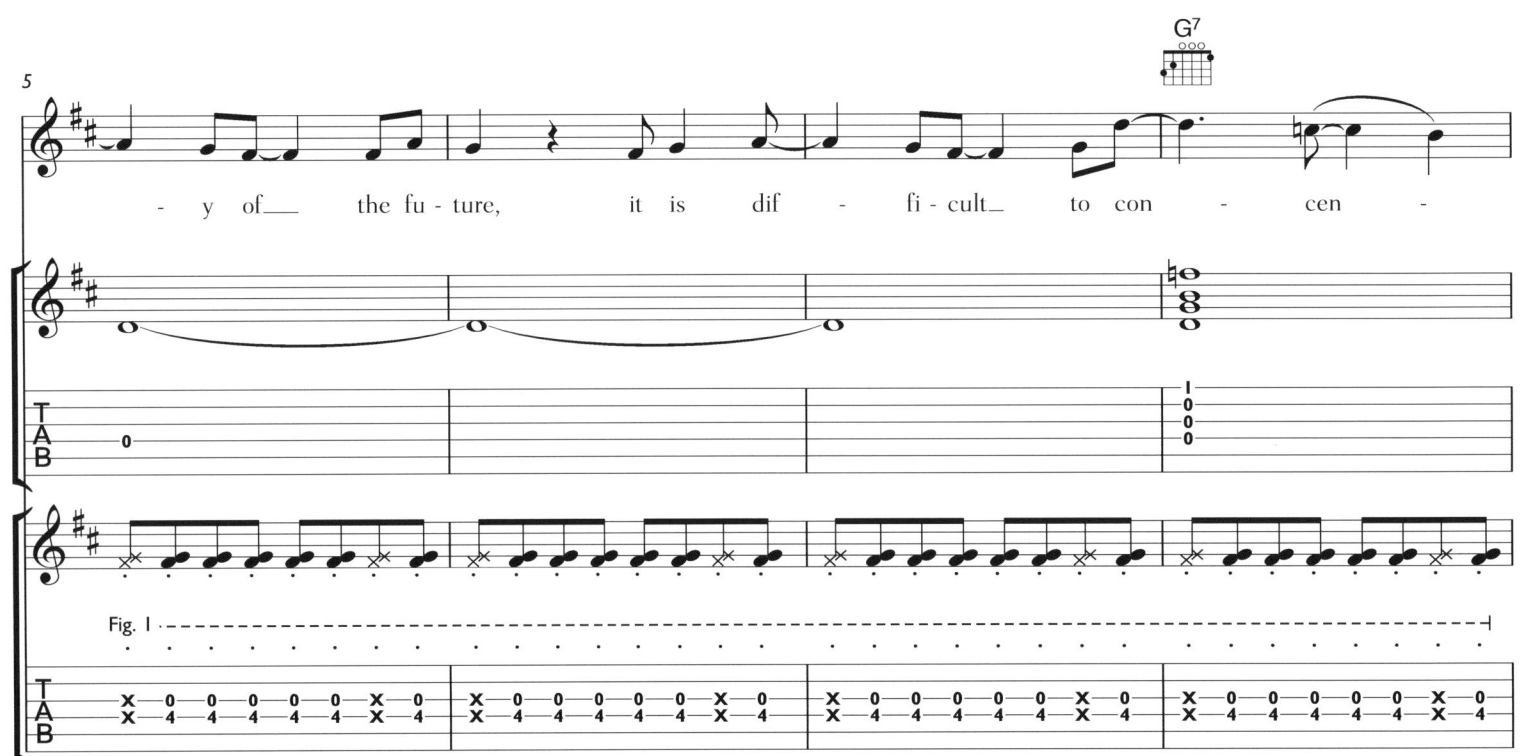

© 1997 Warner/Chappell Music Ltd
All Rights Reserved.

C
Dadd4
3fr
Elec. Gtr. 3 plays Fig. 1 cont. sim.
25
In a cit -
mp
1/2
Bass
mp
G7
C
Elec. Gtr. 1
29
- y of the fu - ture, it is dif - fi - cult to find a space,
Elec. Gtr. 2
mp with fuzz & wah

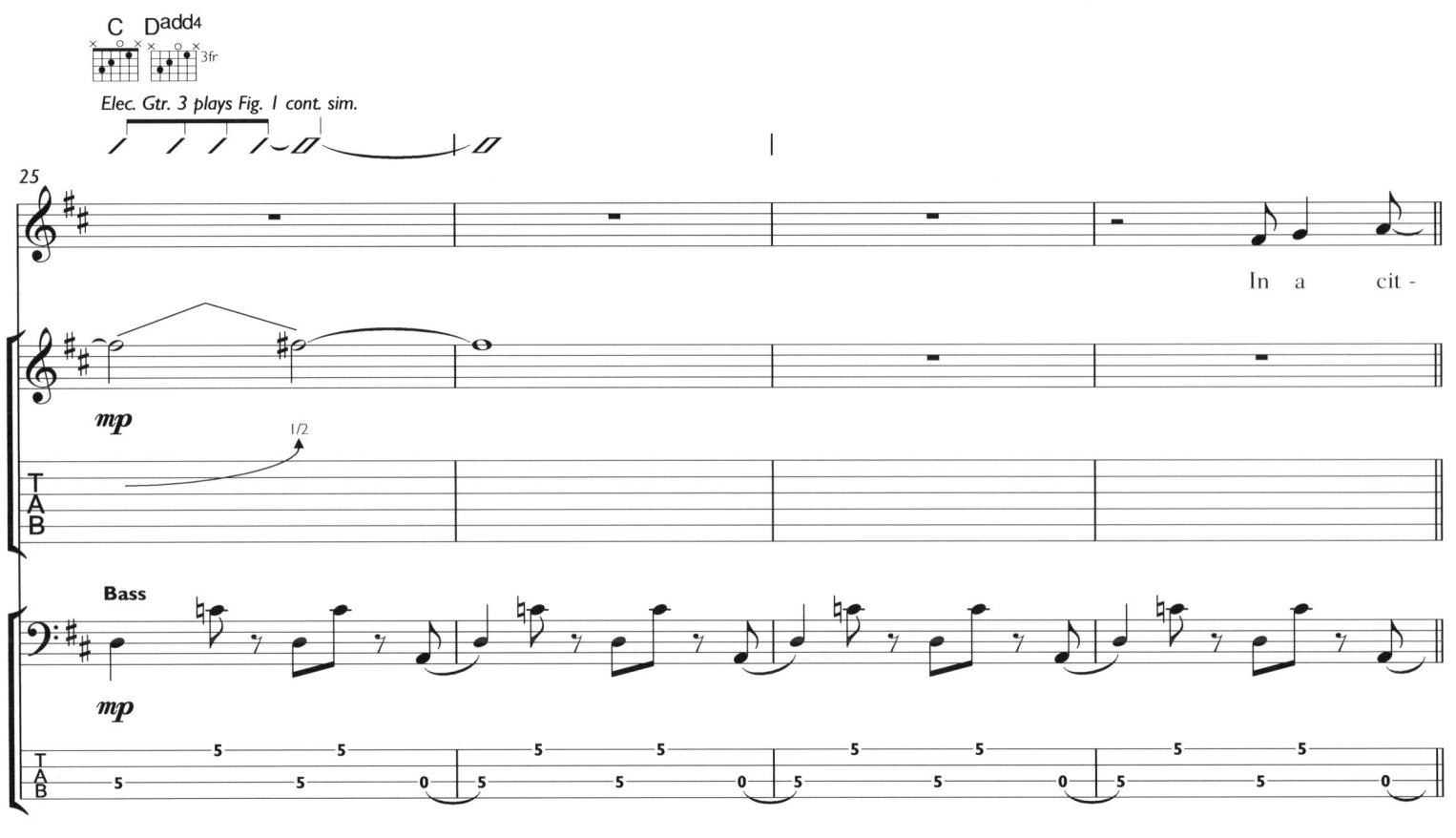

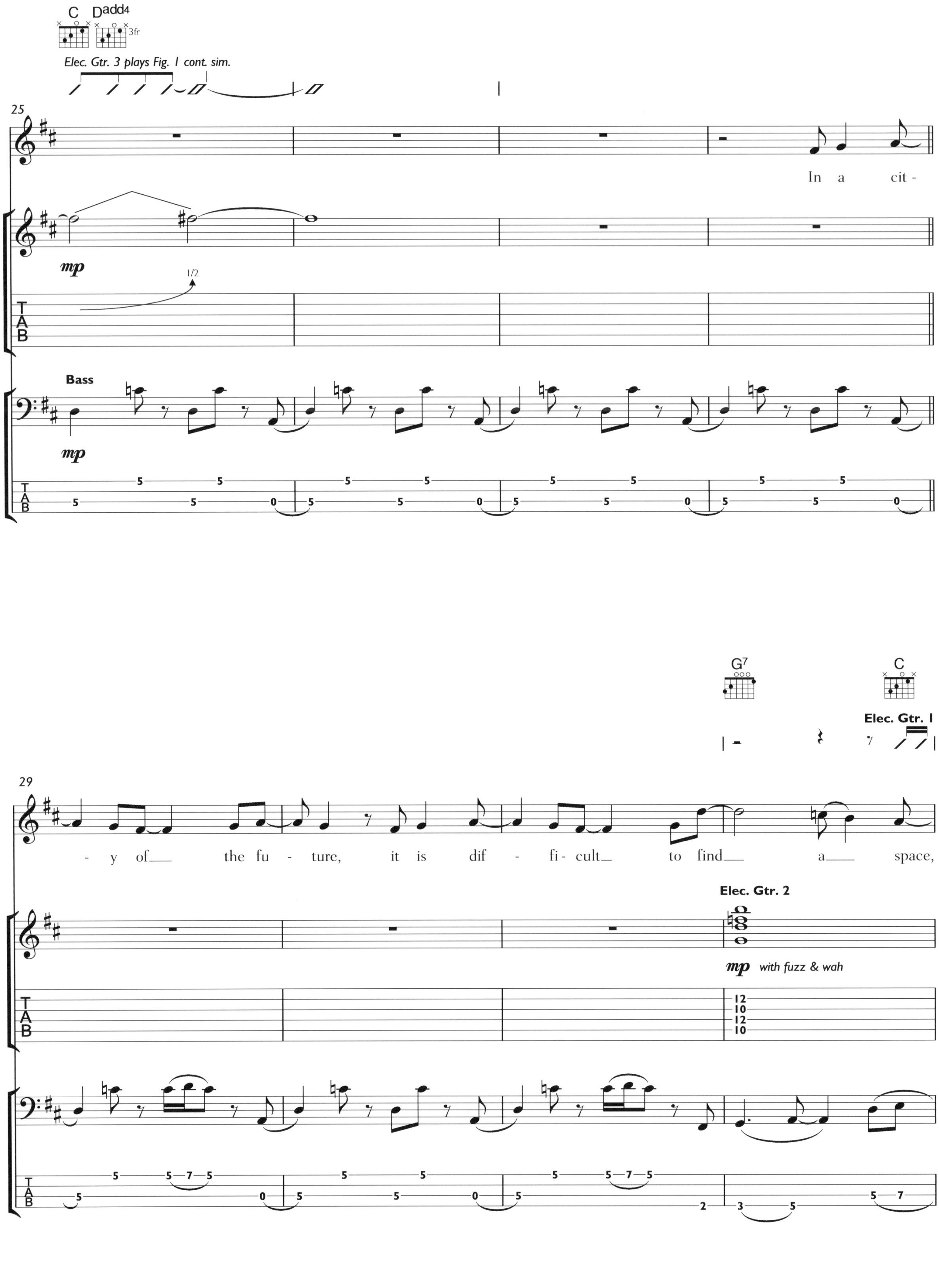

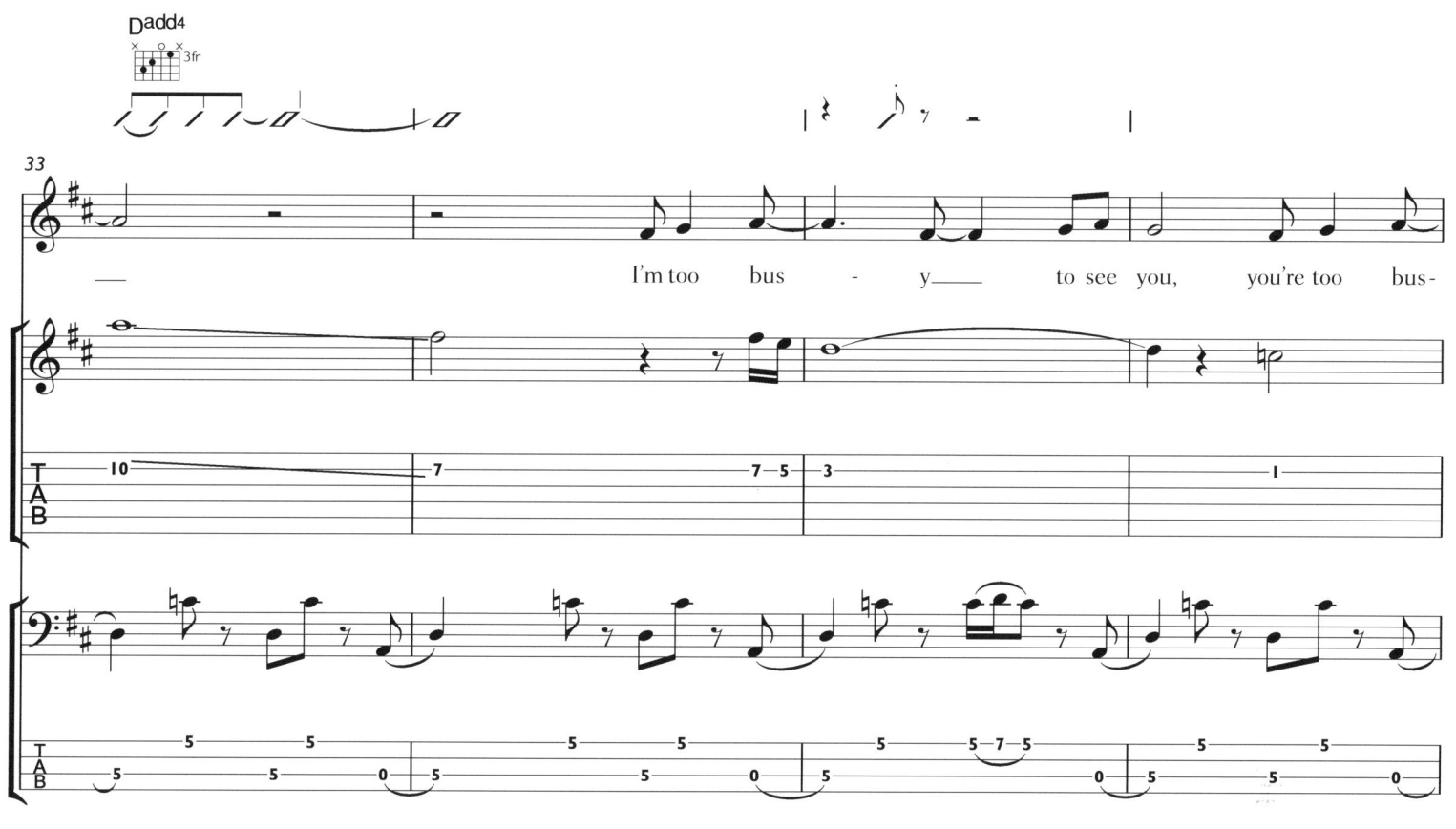

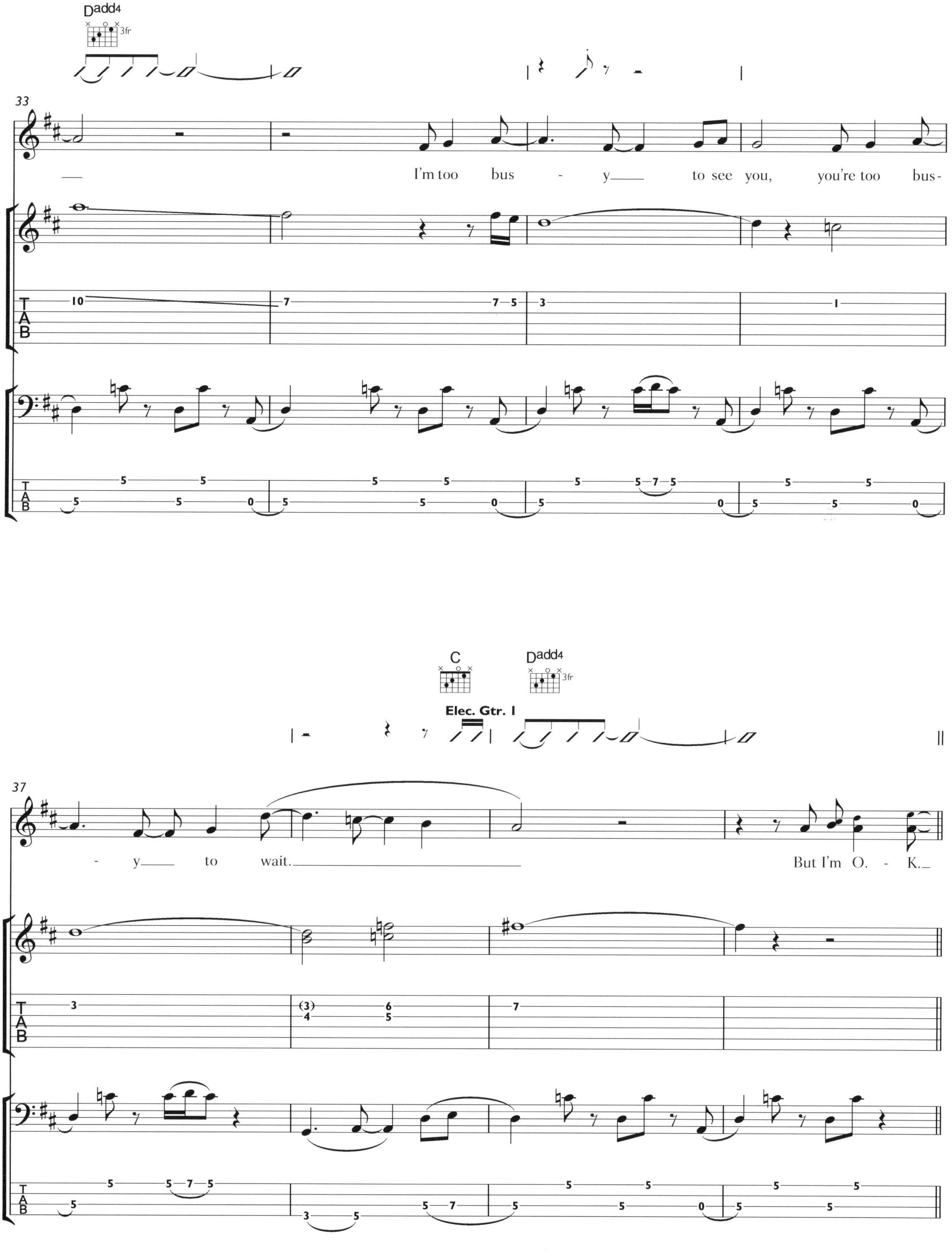
Dadd4
3fr
33
I'm too bus - y to see you, you're too bus-
T
A
B
C
Dadd4
3fr
Elec. Gtr. 1
37
- y to wait.
But I'm O. - K.

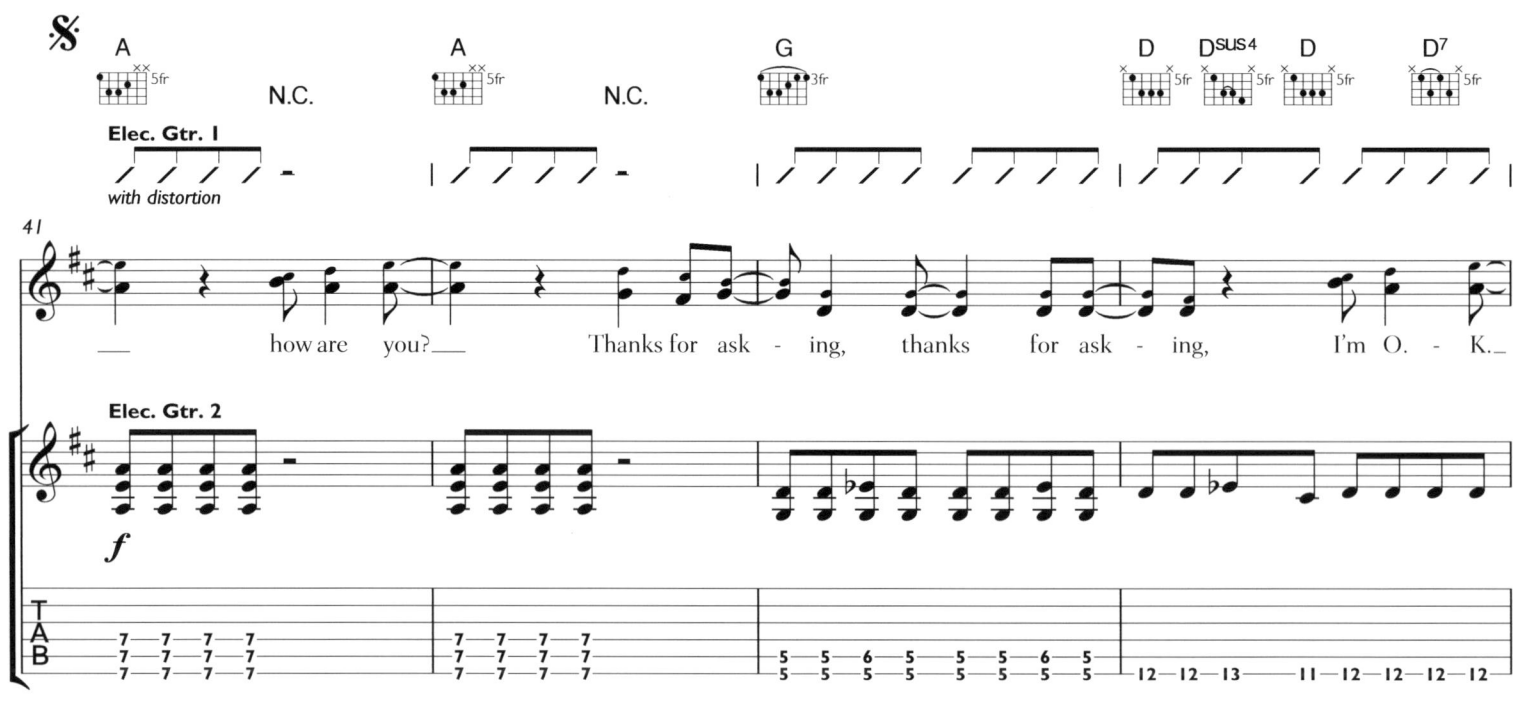

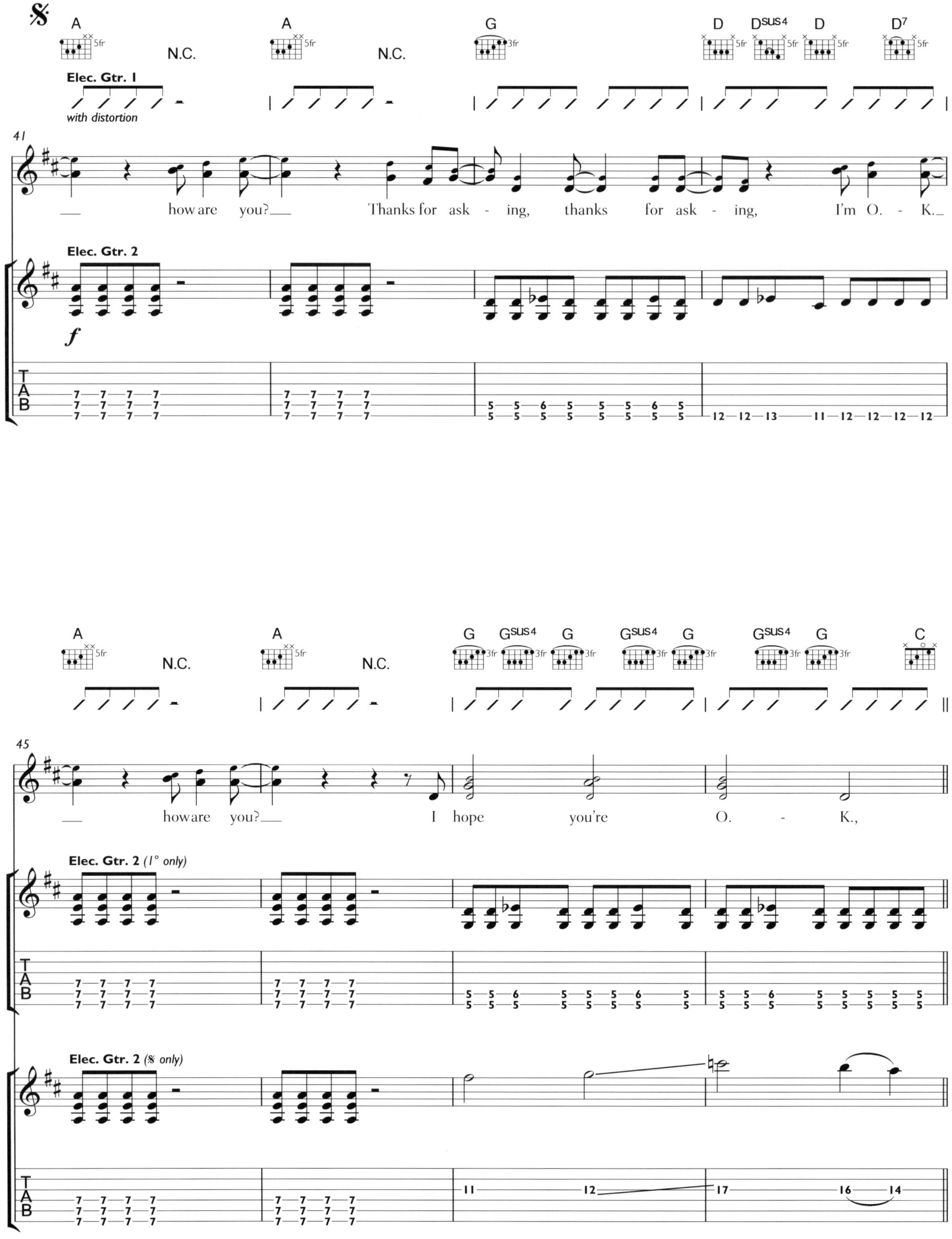
A
N.C.
A
N.C.
G
D
Dsus4
D
D7
Elec. Gtr. 1
with distortion
41
how are you? Thanks for ask - ing, thanks for ask - ing, I'm O. - K.
Elec. Gtr. 2
A
N.C.
A
N.C.
G
Gsus4
G
Gsus4
G
Gsus4
G
C
45
how are you? I hope you're O. - K.,
Elec. Gtr. 2 (1° only)
Elec. Gtr. 2 (𝄋 only)

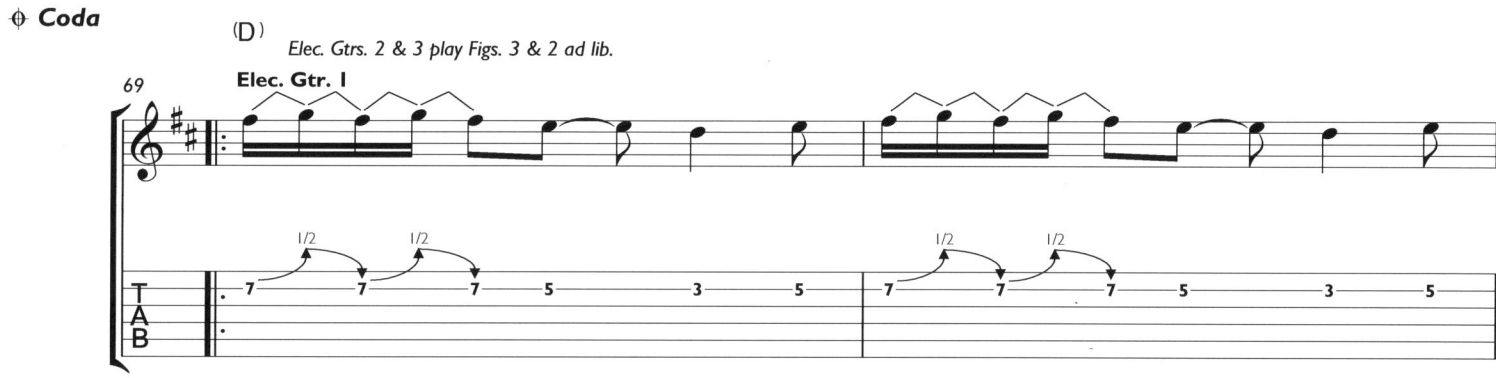
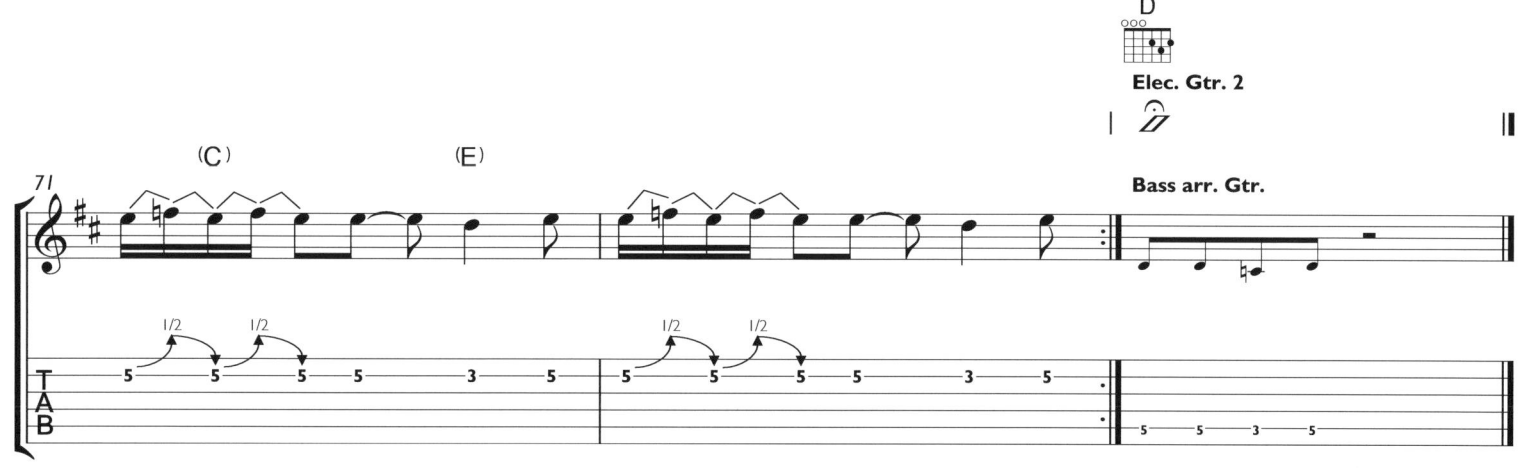

HOW I MADE MY MILLIONS

Words and Music by Thomas Yorke

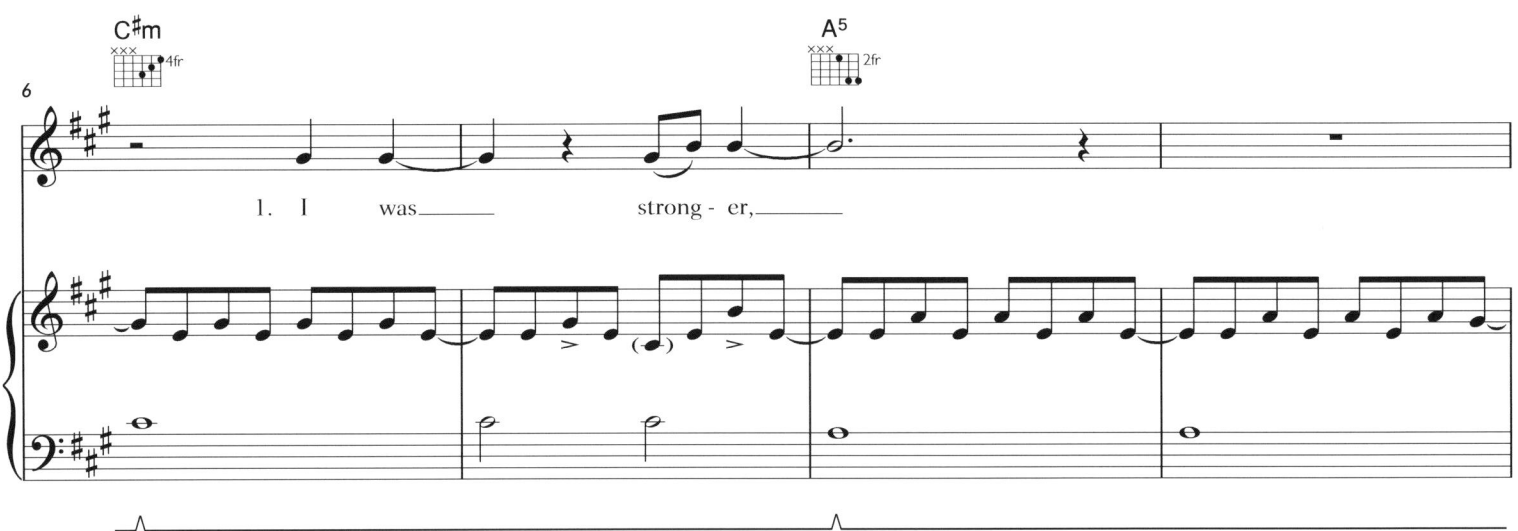

1. I was_____ strong-er,_____

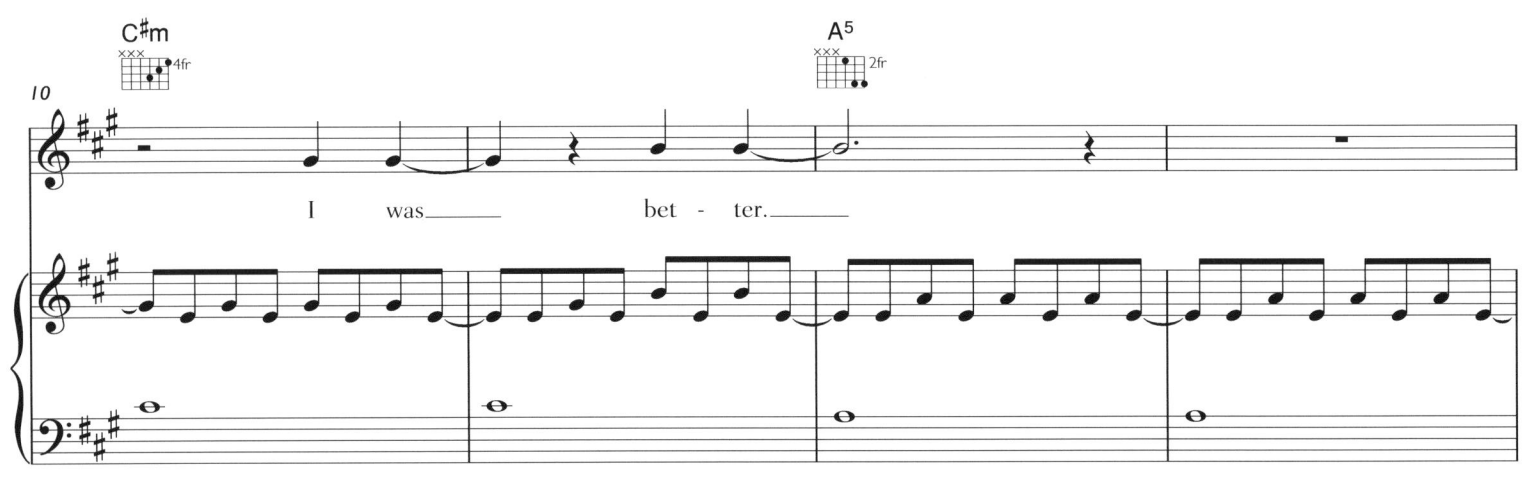

I was_____ bet-ter._____

© 1998 Warner/Chappell Music Ltd
All Rights Reserved.

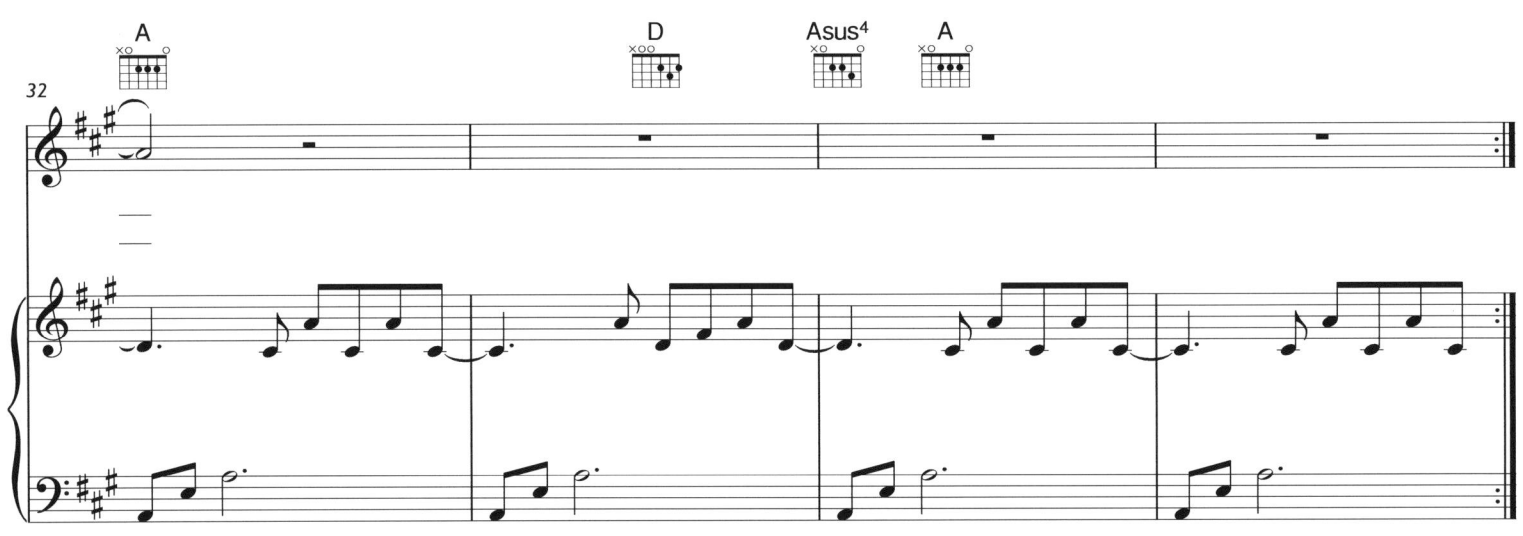
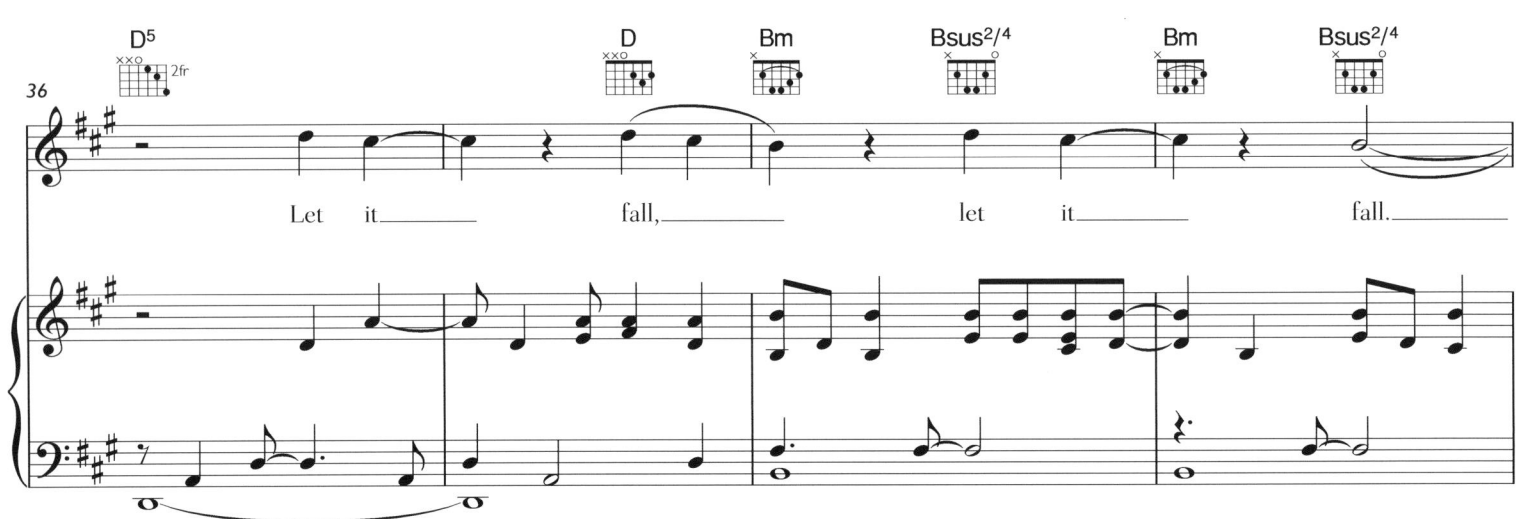

Notation and Tablature explained

Understanding chord boxes

Chord boxes show the neck of your guitar as if viewed head on—the vertical lines represent the strings (low E to high E, from left to right), and the horizontal lines represent the frets.

An **X** above a string means 'don't play this string'.
An **O** above a string means 'play this open string'.
The black dots show you where to put your fingers.

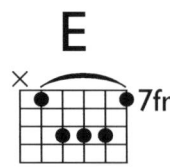

A curved line joining two dots on the fretboard represents a 'barre'. This means that you flatten one of your fingers (usually the first) so that you hold down all the strings between the two dots at the fret marked.

A fret marking at the side of the chord box shows you where chords that are played higher up the neck are located.

Tuning your guitar

The best way to tune your guitar is to use an electronic tuner. Alternatively, you can use relative tuning; this will ensure that your guitar is in tune with itself, but won't guarantee that you will be in tune with the original track (or any other musicians).

How to use relative tuning

Fret the low E string at the 5th fret and pluck; compare this with the sound of the open A string. The two notes should be in tune. If not, adjust the tuning of the A string until the two notes match.

Repeat this process for the other strings according to this diagram:

Note that the B string should match the note at the 4th fret of the G string, whereas all the other strings match the note at the 5th fret of the string below.

As a final check, ensure that the bottom E string and top E string are in tune with each other.

Detuning and Capo use

If the song uses an unconventional tuning, it will say so clearly at the top of the music, e.g. '6 = D' (tune string 6 to D) or 'detune guitar down by a semitone'. If a capo is used, it will tell you the fret number to which it must be attached. The standard notation will always be in the key at which the song sounds, but the guitar tab will take tuning changes into account. Just detune/add the capo and follow the fret numbers. The chord symbols will show the sounding chord above and the chord you actually play below in brackets.

Use of figures

In order to make the layout of scores clearer, figures that occur several times in a song will be numbered, e.g. 'Fig. 1', 'Fig. 2', etc.
A dotted line underneath shows the extent of the 'figure'. When a phrase is to be played, it will be marked clearly in the score, along with the instrument that should play it.

Reading Guitar Tab

Guitar tablature illustrates the six strings of the guitar graphically, showing you where you put your fingers for each note or chord. It is always shown with a stave in standard musical notation above it. The guitar tablature stave has six lines, each of them representing a different string. The top line is the high E string, the second line being the B string, and so on. Instead of using note heads, guitar tab uses numbers which show the fret number to be stopped by the left hand. The rhythm is indicated underneath the tab stave. Ex. 1 (below) shows four examples of single notes.

Ex. 2 shows four different chords. The 3rd one (Asus4) should be played as a barre chord at the 5th fret. The 4th chord (C9) is a half, or jazz chord shape. You have to mute the string marked with an 'x' (the A string in this case) with a finger of your fretting hand in order to obtain the correct voicing.

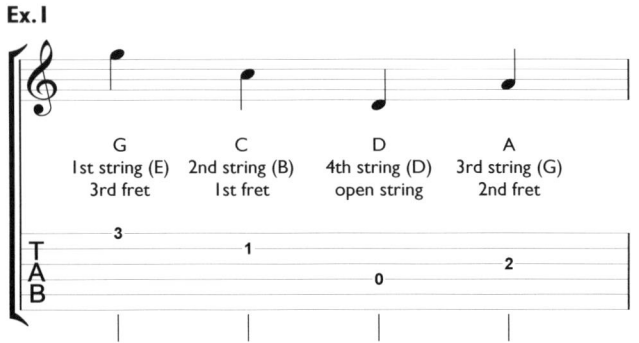

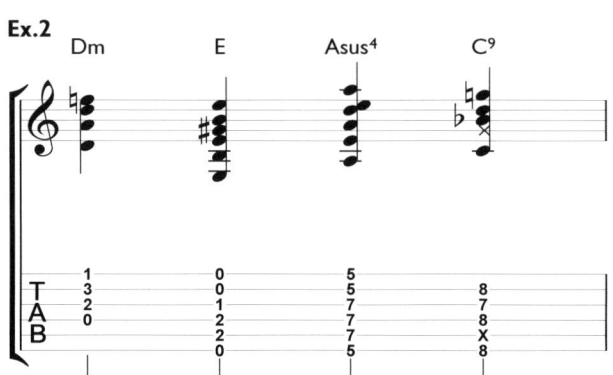

Notation of other guitar techniques

Picking hand techniques:

1. Down and up strokes
These symbols show that the first and third notes are to be played with a down stroke of the pick and the others up strokes.

2. Palm mute
Mute the notes with the palm of the picking hand by lightly touching the strings near the bridge.

3. Pick rake
Drag the pick across the indicated strings with a single sweep. The extra pressure will often mute the notes slightly and accentuate the final note.

4. Arpeggiated chords
Strum across the indicated strings in the direction of the arrow head of the wavy line.

5. Tremolo picking
Shown by the slashes on the stem of the note. Very fast alternate picking. Rapidly and continuously move the pick up and down on each note.

6. Pick scrape
Drag the edge of the pick up or down the lower strings to create a scraping sound.

7. Right hand tapping
'Tap' onto the note indicated by a '+' with a finger of the picking hand. It is nearly always followed by a pull-off to sound the note fretted below.

8. Tap slide
As with tapping, but the tapped note is slid randomly up the fretboard, then pulled off to the following note.

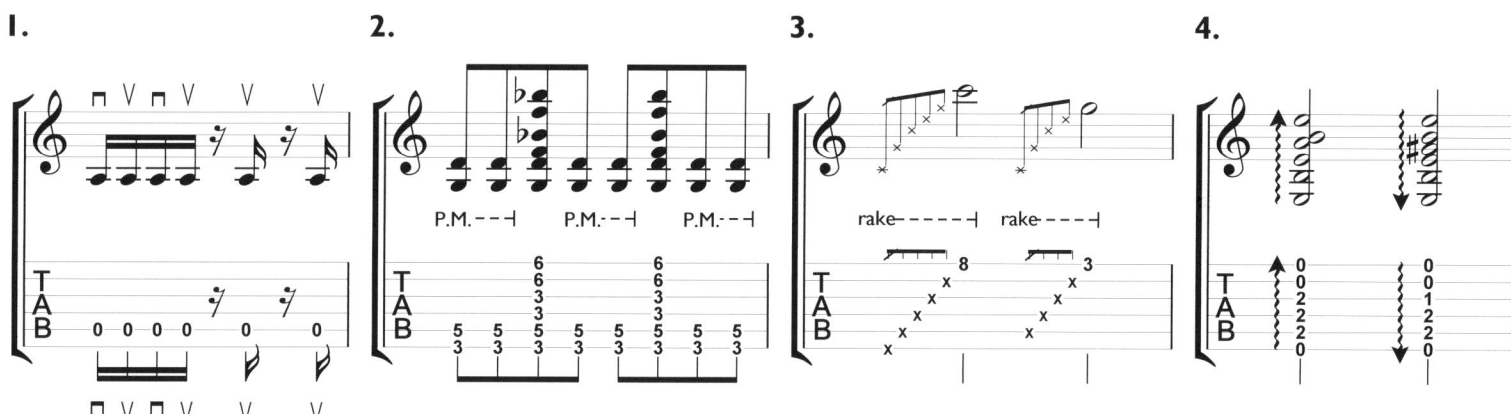

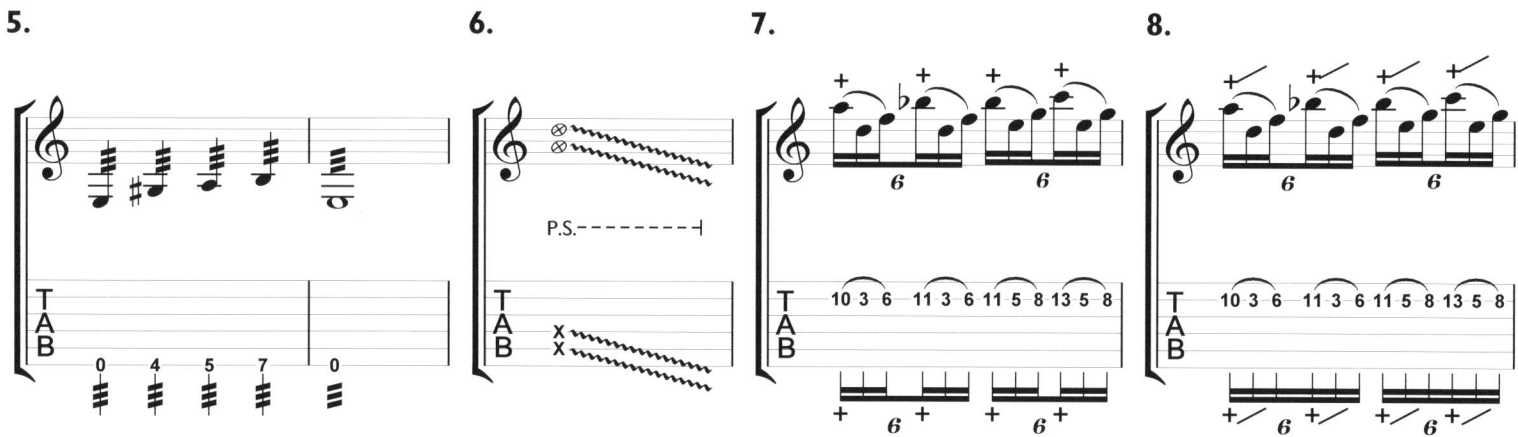

Fretting hand techniques:

1. Hammer-on and pull-off
These consist of two or more notes linked together by a slur. For hammer-ons, fret and play the lowest note, then 'hammer on' to the higher note with another finger. For a pull-off, play the highest note then 'pull off' to a lower note fretted with another finger. In both cases, only pick the first note.

2. Glissandi (slides)
Fret and pick the first note, then slide the finger up to the second note. If they are slurred together, do not re-pick the second note.

3. Slow glissando
Play the note(s) and slowly slide the finger(s) in the direction of the diagonal line(s).

4. Quick glissando
Play the note(s) and immediately slide the finger(s) in the direction of the diagonal line(s).

5. Trills
Play the note and rapidly alternate between this note and the nearest one above in the key signature. If a note in brackets is shown before, begin with this note.

6. Fret hand muting
Mute the notes with cross noteheads with the fretting hand.

7. Left hand tapping
Sound the note by tapping or hammering on to the note indicated by a '°' with a finger of the fretting hand.

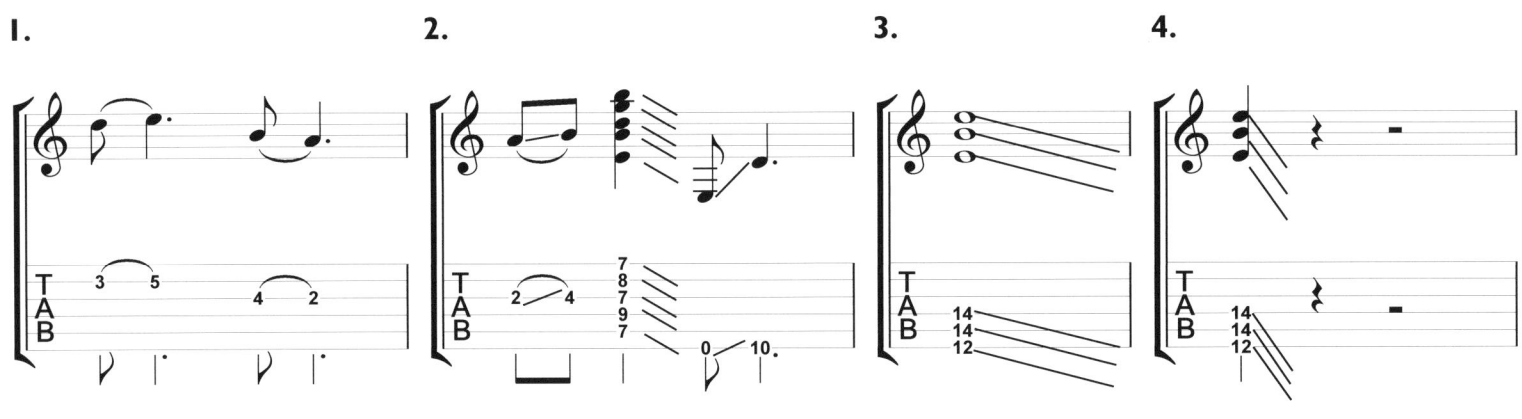

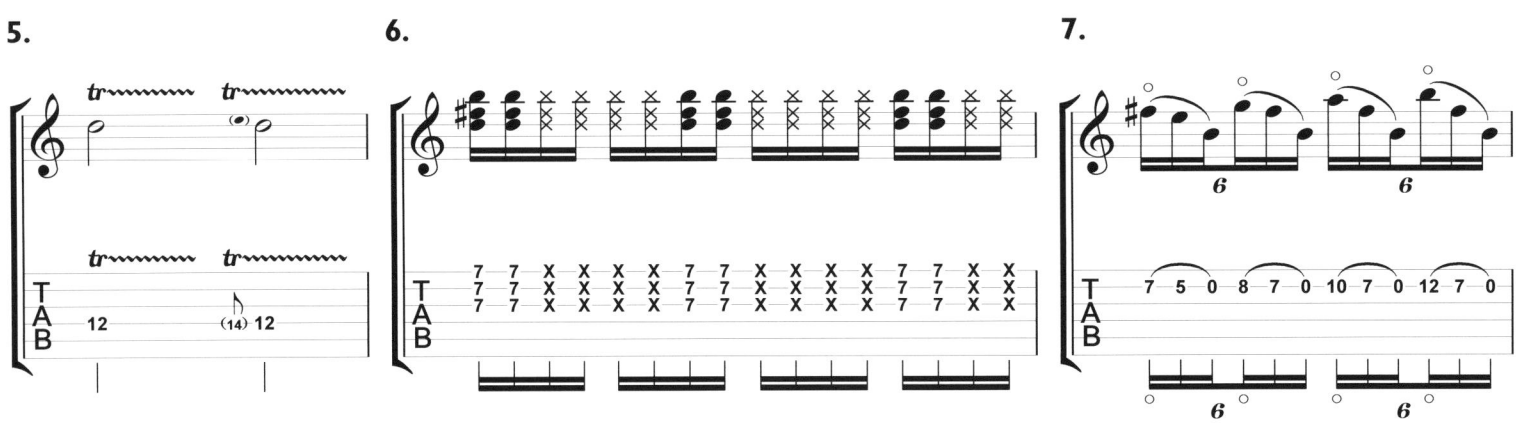

Bends and vibrato

Bends
Bends are shown by the curved arrow pointing to a number (in the tab).
Fret the first note and then bend the string up by the amount shown.

1. Semitone bend (half step bend)
The smallest conventional interval; equivalent to raising the note by one fret.

2. Whole tone bend (whole step bend)
Equivalent to two frets.

3. Minor third bend (whole step and a half)
Equivalent to three frets.

4. Microtonal bend (quarter-tone bend, Blues curl)
Bend by a slight degree, roughly equivalent to half a fret.

5. Bend and release
Fret and pick the first note. Bend up for the length of the note shown. May be followed by a release—letting the string fall back down to the original pitch.

6. Ghost bend (prebend)
Fret the bracketed note and bend quickly before picking the note.

7. Reverse bend
Fret the bracketed note and bend quickly before picking the note, immediately let fall back to the original.

8. Multiple bends
A series of bends and releases joined together. Only pick the first note.

9. Unison bend
Strike both indicated notes simultaneously and immediately bend the lower string up to the same pitch as the higher one.

10. Double note bend
Play both notes and bend simultaneously by the amount shown.

11. Bend involving more than one note
Bend first note and hold the bend whilst striking a note on another string.

12. Bends involving stationary notes
Play notes and bend lower string. Hold until release is indicated.

13. Vibrato
Shown by a wavy line. The fretting hand creates a vibrato effect using small, rapid up and down bends.

14. Bend and tap technique
Play and bend notes as shown, then sound final pitch by tapping onto note as indicated.

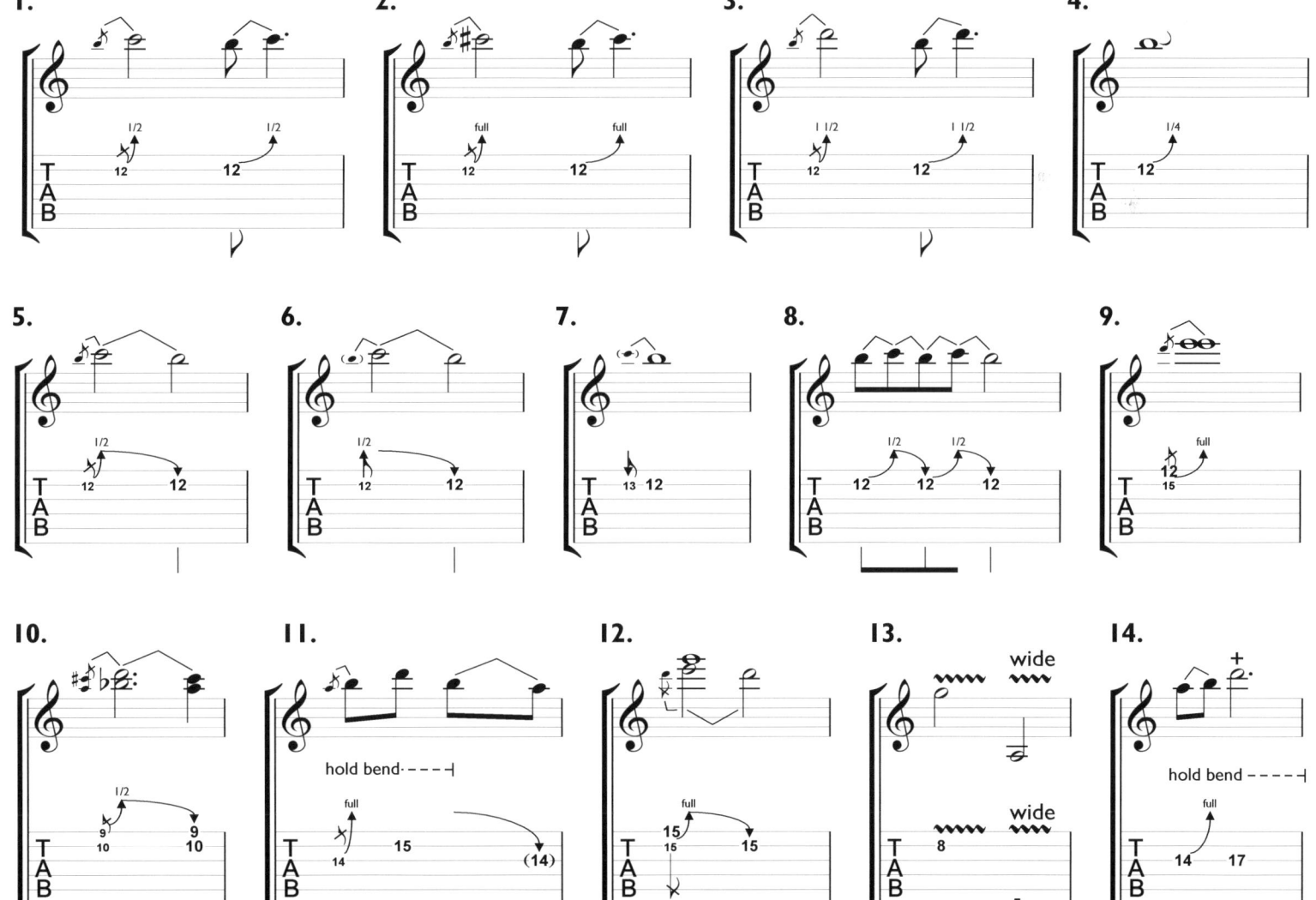

Tremolo arm (wammy bar)

1. Vibrato with tremolo arm
Create vibrato using small, rapid inflections of the tremolo arm.

2. Tremolo arm dive and return
Play note and depress tremolo arm by degree shown. Release arm to return to original note.

3. Tremolo arm scoop
Depress the arm just before picking the note and release.

4. Tremolo arm dip (or doop)
Pick the note, then lower the arm and quickly release.

5. Sustained note and dive bomb
Play note, hold for length of time shown and then depress arm to lower the pitch until the strings go slack.

6. Gargle
Pick the note and flick the tremolo arm rapidly with the same hand, making the pitch quiver.

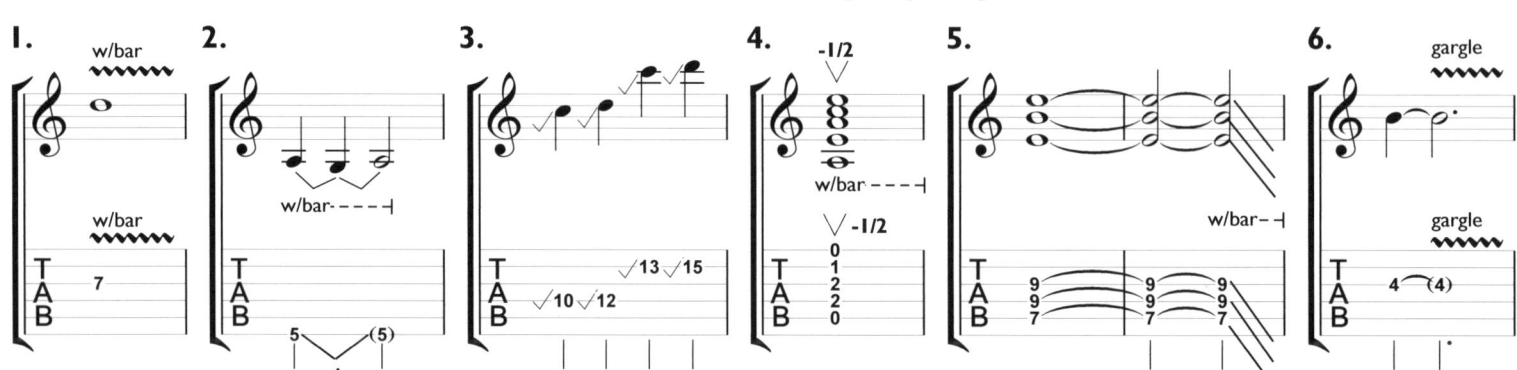

Harmonics & Other techniques

1. Natural harmonics
Instead of fretting properly, touch the string lightly with the fretting hand at the fret shown in the tab. Pick as normal. Diamond noteheads show the resultant pitch.

2. Artificial harmonics
The first tab number is fretted and held with the fretting hand as normal. The picking hand then produces a harmonic by using a finger to touch the string lightly at the fret shown by the bracketed number. Pick with another finger of the picking hand.

3. Pinched harmonics
Fret the note as shown, but create a harmonic by digging into the string with the side of the thumb as you pick it.

4. Tapped harmonics
Fret the note as shown, but create the harmonic through tapping lightly with the picking hand at the fret shown in brackets.

5. Touch harmonics
Fret the first note, hold it, then touch the string lightly at the fret shown at the end of the slur with the picking hand.

6. Violining
Turn the volume control to zero, pick the notes and then turn the control to fade the note in smoothly.

7. Fingering (fretting hand)
Small numbers show the finger with which each note is to be fretted.

8. Fingerpicking notation (PIMA)
Notation that shows which finger should be used to pick each note when playing finger style. p = thumb, i = index, m = middle, a = ring.

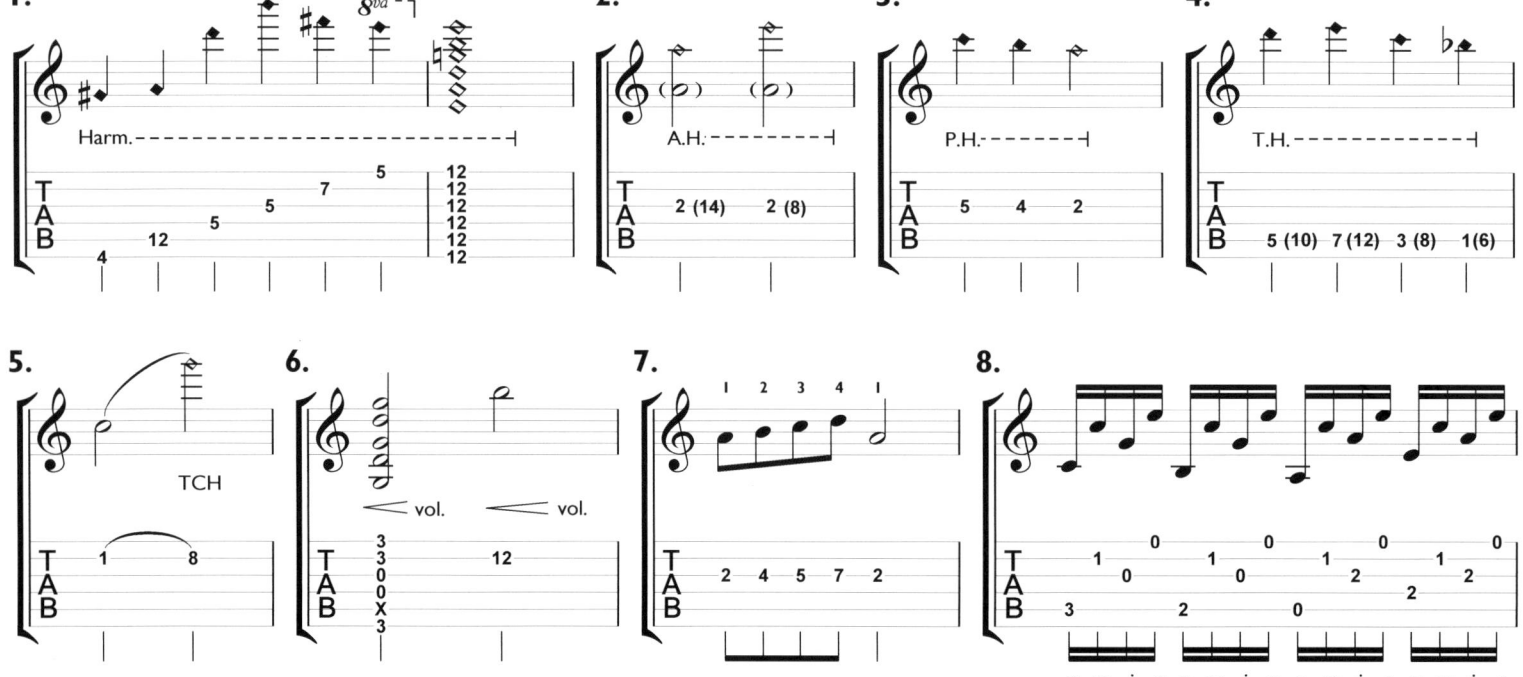